"Old walls with slick no bills chalked on them spilt behind
Aboard stood in a field; Come to Blackpool.

Queer ~~Motorcycles~~ Fine motorcycles whizzed by or splashed past us: a Zenith
Gradua, a Rudge-Multi, wi[...] two
Sunbeams with laminated spring forks. I watched for the blue
Indian, an ~~old~~ American make, which we usually encountered at
nine fifteen in Upton, just before reaching the Clegg Arms.
I had never got rid of the childhood impression that its rider
was somehow identified with the machine, that together it was a real
Indian who lived somewhere in a hollow.

Then, occasionally, a thing would approach us, seeming at
first less like a ~~motorbyke~~ motorcycle than a terrestrial visitor; a pre
war Bat or Roc, of enormous length with open belt drive and
~~goatshorn~~ racing handlebars, over which its goggled rider crouched
flat on the tank. With unearthly explosions, ~~the Bats, the Rocs~~ they
voyaged into the gloom: discarded experiments, as I see them now,
of the Industrial Revolution, obsolescent monuments to foundered
genius.-

~~Now we were~~ As we left Upton, Leaving Upton, and the blue Indian ~~came~~ slanted by, a
little late today: ~~Almost half-past~~ almost nine-thirty. Featherstonhaugh turned
his head a fraction so that I could see the slight, ~~[already~~
~~fading,]~~ smile on his lips, ~~&~~ a signal. But his impassive ~~mein~~ mien
reassembled itself instantly. Approaching the Birkenhead docksid
the pubs came thick and fast, ~~[now]~~ here with sea-sounding names: the
Dolphin, ~~(the)~~ Blue Peter, the ~~Black Pan~~ Right whale. Funnels appeared over
~~sheds of the~~ sheds of the Ellerman line; the crosstrees of a windjammer.
Smells of cordage were in our nostrils. Sirens wailed. Twice
nightly continuous performance, an advertisement for the Hippo-
drome said, 6:30 and 8:30: Little Tich, ~~Harry Champion~~. While
the Argyle announced ~~Herschel Henlere~~ Harry Champion, ~~Harry Welden~~, Brown's
Bioscope. It was melancholy to be bidding adieu to these familia
placards which were like friends.

Edward Burra

Cian Quayle

Julian Cooper

Alberto Rebollo

Ailsa Cox

Annick Drösdal-Levillain

Ross Birrell and David Harding

Robert Sheppard

Jorge Martínez García

Malcolm Lowry

Adrian Henri

Ian McMillan

Colin Dilnot

Paul Rooney

Michele Gemelos

Cisco Jiménez

Mark Goodall

Pete Flowers

FROM THE MERSEY TO THE WORLD

Nicholas Murray

Michael Turner

Ray Lowry

Gordon Bowker

Brian O'Toole

Edited by
Bryan Biggs and Helen Tookey

First published 2009 by
Liverpool University Press
4 Cambridge Street
Liverpool
L69 7ZU

and

the Bluecoat
School Lane
Liverpool
L1 3BX

British Library Cataloguing-in-Publication data
A British Library CIP record is available

Every effort has been made to contact the holders of
copyright material reproduced in this book. The publishers
would be grateful to be informed of any errors or omissions
for correction in future editions.

ISBN 978-1-84631-228-1

Designed by AW @ www.axisgraphicdesign.co.uk
Printed and bound by Gutenberg Press, Malta

COVER
Malcolm Lowry reclining in a deck chair at Dollarton, 1945 (University of
British Columbia Library, Rare Books and Special Collections, Malcolm
Lowry Collection, BC 1614/07) Photo of the Dee Estuary by Colin Dilnot

HALF-TITLE PAGE
Manuscript page from first draft of 'Enter One in Sumptuous Armour'
(University of British Columbia Library, Rare Books and Special
Collections, Malcolm Lowry Collection, BC Box 11, File 11)

TITLE PAGE
Photo by Colin Dilnot

PAGES 38-39, 90-91, 114-115, 160
Telegrams and letter relating to Lowry from 1938–40 reproduced by
permission of Liverpool Record Office (920 LOW)

Contents

Malcolm Lowry passport photo, 1946

University of British Columbia Library, Rare Books and Special Collections,
Malcolm Lowry Collection, BC 1614/20

Malcolm Lowry
Late of the Bowery
His prose was flowery
And often glowery
He lived, nightly, and drank, daily
And died, playing the ukulele.

Malcolm Lowry, self-penned 'epitaph'

Introduction

'The voyage that never ends':
Malcolm Lowry – from the Mersey to the world

Outward bound

On 12 May 1927, under the headline 'Deckhand with a ukulele: schoolboy's world search for inspiration', the *Liverpool Echo* reported that a 'seventeen-year-old son of a Liverpool cotton broker', Malcolm Lowry by name, was forsaking the comforts of his home at Inglewood, Caldy, overlooking the River Dee, for a rigorous life at sea, shipping as a deckhand at £2.10s a month on the steamer SS *Pyrrhus* bound for 'the Far East, calling at Port Said, Shanghai, and possibly Yokohama'. In the first chapter of his masterpiece, the 1947 novel *Under the Volcano*, in a portrait of the Wirral setting of his youth, Lowry would recall: 'The smoke of freighters outward bound from Liverpool hung low on the horizon'. *Outward* bound: at the age of seventeen, eager to 'see something of the world', as the *Echo* report put it, Lowry already evinced what Malcolm Bradbury would later describe as a 'curious internationalism'.[1]
Yet at the same time he retained always in his mind, and in his writing, the psychogeography of his early years by the Mersey: the topography, both accurately real and thoroughly symbolic, of his Wirral 'Eden' and its dark twin, Liverpool, 'that terrible city whose main street is the ocean'.[2]

Lowry's departure on board the *Pyrrhus* marked the beginning of what he would later describe, in a characteristically brilliant pun, as his 'tooloose Lowry-trek':[3] thirty years of voyaging – geographically, psychologically and creatively – that would take in two marriages, three continents, several jails, a couple of psychiatric hospitals, and a squatter's shack; and would leave in its wake both thousands of empty bottles and hundreds of thousands of words, including arguably one of the greatest twentieth-century novels in English. The confused, and still confusing, end of the voyage, in an obscure village in East Sussex, would be (mis)reported by another English provincial newspaper, this time the *Brighton Argus*:

> One evening last week Mrs Marjorie [actually Margerie] Lowry, of Ripe
> [in fact White] Cottage, Ripe, tried to stop her 47-year-old writer-husband,
> Clarence [Lowry's first name], from starting on the gin. She smashed the
> bottle on the floor. And he hit her. Afraid, Mrs Lowry fled next door, and did

---

1   Malcolm Bradbury, review of *Hear Us O Lord from Heaven Thy Dwelling Place* and *Under the Volcano*, *Critical Quarterly*, 4.4 (1962), pp. 377–79.
2   Malcolm Lowry, 'The Forest Path to the Spring', in *Hear Us O Lord from Heaven Thy Dwelling Place & Lunar Caustic* (London: Picador, 1991), p. 226.
3   He uses the phrase in a letter to John Davenport, written from Oaxaca in 1936 at a very low point of his life. In *Selected Letters of Malcolm Lowry*, ed. Harvey Breit and Margerie Bonner Lowry (London: Penguin, 1985), p. 13.

not go back to the cottage until nine o'clock the next morning. When she did she found her husband dead.[4]

It's probably safe to say that the 47-year-old writer-husband would have been tickled by the melodramatic style and by the many inaccuracies of this report, and would have made it the basis for a short story, which would inexorably have grown into a novella and then a full-scale epic novel, itself part of a vast over-arching scheme involving multiple works and multiple genres, all subject to endless revisions and the working-in of new levels of symbolism. The perfectly apt title Lowry gave to just such a scheme for his writings, left uncompleted at his death, was 'the voyage that never ends'.

Fluctuating fortunes: Liverpool, city of the sea

In 2009, a hundred years on from Lowry's birth, it is appropriate that his centenary is being celebrated in the port from which he embarked on his endless voyage.[5] Two years before Lowry was born, Liverpool was celebrating the seven hundredth anniversary of its founding. The city was at its commercial peak, second city of the British Empire behind London, its reach truly global. Cargo, material and human, passed through its docks in a never-ending flow and it was the most significant European port of emigration: of the 5.5 million passengers bound for America between 1860 and 1900 for instance, 4.75 million of them passed through Liverpool.[6] In 1907 Walter Dixon Scott described the Landing Stage, the symbolic focus of Liverpool's maritime connections to the rest of the world and a place of social interaction for the city's diverse population, as a 'democratic promenade'.[7] Here, the world appeared to be 'in one city'.[8] And here too fortunes were being made. Toxteth-born Arthur Lowry's prosperity as a broker in the Liverpool Cotton Exchange enabled him to move in 1894 'over the water' to the Wirral, where his youngest – and most troublesome – son Clarence Malcolm was born fifteen years later. Maritime business provided the family's wealth, and the sea, as Lowry's first biographer Douglas Day has pointed out, became one of the writer's 'prime symbols, more important even than alcohol'.[9]

Merseyside was, in the early decades of the twentieth century, far from the cultural backwater that Lowry's desire to get away might suggest. When he rehearsed his escape from his roots on the SS *Pyrrhus* in 1927, it was possible to access in Liverpool and the Wirral the two most modern and popular creative expressions, cinema and jazz, which Lowry was to embrace so enthusiastically. That year Carl Gustav Jung

---

4   Cited in Gordon Bowker, *Pursued by Furies: A Life of Malcolm Lowry* (London: HarperCollins, 1993), p. 602.

5   To be strictly accurate, Lowry sailed from Birkenhead docks. It is Liverpool, however, that stands in his writing as the symbolic 'point of departure' and archetypal port city.

6   John Belchem (ed.), *Liverpool 800: Culture, Character and History* (Liverpool: Liverpool University Press, 2006), p. 14.

7   Walter Dixon Scott, *Liverpool 1907* (Neston: Gallery Press, 1979 [1907]), p. 39.

8   The slogan adopted for Liverpool's (successful) bid to become European Capital of Culture in 2008 was 'the world in one city'.

9   Douglas Day, *Malcolm Lowry: A Biography* (Oxford: Oxford University Press, 1973), p. 94.

8

TOP
SS *Pyrrhus* entering Birkenhead Docks

BOTTOM
Marine Lake, West Kirby

RIGHT
The young Lowry in golfing attire, taken from the *Liverpool Echo*,
12 May 1927

British Library

THURSDAY, MAY 12, 1927.

DECKHAND WITH A UKULELE.

SCHOOLBOY'S WORLD SEARCH FOR INSPIRATION.

Fresh from Leys College, Cambridge, Malcolm Lowry, the seventeen-year-old son of a Liverpool cotton broker, sails from Liverpool on Saturday as a deckhand, at £2 10s a month, in the steamer Pyrrhus, which is going on a tramp voyage to the Far East, calling at Port Said, Shanghai, and possibly Yokohama.

Young Lowry, who lives with his parents at Inglewood, Caldy, Cheshire, told an " Echo " representative, to-day, that he desires to see something of the world and gain some experience of life before going to the university.

" The voyage will last eight to ten months," he said, " and during that time

Malcolm Lowry.

I shall work just the same as the other members of the crew. I shall not receive—and I don't want—any privileges.

WRITING AND COMPOSING.

" The work will keep me fit, and will be a good thing for me. As I write short stories and compose dance music I hope to get fresh atmosphere and inspiration."

" I shall take my ukulele with me, and when off watch shall try to think out some new dance tunes. Ronald Hill, a school chum of mine, and I have written several Charlestons, one of which, ' Three Little Doggone Mice ' (as mentioned in the " Echo " dancing notes some weeks ago), has already been published.

" Other dance tunes we have composed are ' Hindoo Babe,' ' You Got to Play Hot Rhythm,' ' Dream Man's a'Coming on a Train of Stars,' ' Dismal Swamp,' ' Dunnohow Blues,' and ' I've Said Good-bye to Shanghai.' "

Lowry, who won the Hoylake Boys' Golf Championship in 1925 is a brother of W. M. Lowry, the Birkenhead Park and international Rugby player.

famously dreamt of Liverpool as the 'Pool of Life',[10] and the Bluecoat Society of Arts was formally established as the UK's first arts centre (in a building that had already hosted Roger Fry's seminal Post-Impressionist exhibition in 1911, featuring works by Picasso, Matisse and Cézanne).[11]

And yet, despite this cosmopolitanism, signs of the port's imminent decline and fall were already present. 'By 1914 the high peak of achievement had been reached and passed',[12] and the consequences of a slowdown in trade were profound for a city so dependent on its maritime mercantile status. Subsequent decades witnessed large-scale deindustrialisation and depopulation, with the spiral of economic decline becoming unstoppable after the Second World War. The predominant image of the city, particularly fuelled by the media during the 1970s and 1980s, became one of high unemployment, strikes, crime, maverick politicians, social despair – a city beyond redemption.

Today Liverpool appears to have turned the corner. With substantial assistance from the European Regional Development Fund and other regeneration schemes, its transformation over the past decade from European 'basket case' to cosmopolitan tourist destination has been remarkable. The extent to which this recovery, enabled by public agencies effectively propping up an ailing infrastructure and by private investment in the city's retail heart, is real or illusory will become apparent as the cold winds of recession start to bite. However, Liverpool's repositioning as a genuine world city has been impressive: now a UNESCO World Heritage site, home to national institutions such as Tate Liverpool and National Museums Liverpool, and designated European Capital of Culture 2008, Liverpool is experiencing culture as a significant driver for regeneration. One of the city's strengths, particularly through the latter part of the twentieth century, was its sense of itself as a creative city, spawning writers and poets, comedians and actors, visual artists and musicians. It was the Beatles whose phenomenal global success focused attention on the city as a creative crucible in the 1960s. Yet Malcolm Lowry rarely figures as a 'Liverpool' or even a North West England writer. Possibly his very 'curious internationalism' – the fact that he left England for Europe, then America, Mexico and Canada – has contributed to this uncertainty about where to place him. Our aim in this book is twofold: to restore Lowry to his rightful place as a writer absolutely grounded in the North West of England – Wirral, the Mersey, Liverpool and the Isle of Man – and to explore the other points on his compass: to show how his psychogeography 'flows' in two directions.

By happy coincidence, one of the best known second-hand bookshops in Liverpool owes its existence to Lowry, for it was the discovery of a 1933 first edition copy of

10   Carl Gustav Jung, *Memories, Dreams, Reflections* (London: Collins Fountain Books, 1977 [1963]), p. 224.

11   See R. F. Bisson, *The Sandon Studios Society and the Arts* (Liverpool: Parry Books, 1965), pp. 61–62.

12   Francis Hyde, *Liverpool and the Mersey* (Newton Abbot, 1971), p. 141, quoted in Tony Lane, *Liverpool, City of the Sea* (Liverpool: Liverpool University Press, 1997 [first published as *Liverpool, Gateway to Empire* (London: Lawrence and Wishart, 1987)]), p. 14.

Lowry's first novel, *Ultramarine*, some thirty years ago that provided funds for former merchant seaman Gerard Fitzpatrick to set up Reid of Liverpool. He acquired the book, complete with original dustjacket and review copy note from publishers Jonathan Cape, for just twenty pence in Wallasey on the Wirral, and – on realising the treasure he had unwittingly acquired – sold it for £1,000, with which he set up the bookshop, still going strong on Mount Pleasant.

'For I was born in Liverpool': Lowry's North West

In his poem 'Villaknell', Lowry harks back again to those outward-bound freighters: 'Or on Pier Head my heels I'd cool / Gazing at freighters far away / For I was born in Liverpool'.[13] In fact, he wasn't born in Liverpool, but in New Brighton on the Wirral peninsula on the other side of the Mersey. But it is Liverpool, the great port city, that represents for Lowry the point of departure for all voyages, both literal and metaphorical: describing sailing into Curaçao in 'Through the Panama', he writes, 'There is a more enormous sense of sea and ships in Curaçao than in any other part of the world I know, except Liverpool'.[14] At the same time, Liverpool also stands for the 'city of dreadful night'. In the same story, Lowry's protagonist Sigbjørn Wilderness quotes a horrified description of Panama by 'some Englishman': 'it would be difficult to find elsewhere on the earth's surface a place in which so much villainy and disease and moral and physical abomination were concentrated'. The writer had, Wilderness concludes, 'evidently not lived in Liverpool'.[15] In some ways, Lowry shares the characteristically modernist vision of the city as at one and the same time the font of all life, power and dynamism, and the fearful source of all dirt, squalor and depravity, a terrible vision of moral decay, of 'fallen' human society; half-comically, Lowry's protagonist in the short story 'Present Estate of Pompeii' muses that Pompeii 'at first sight had looked to him a bit like the ruins of Liverpool on a Sunday afternoon'.[16] In the topography of his Canadian idyll at Dollarton, on an inlet close to Vancouver – which, as Annick Drösdal-Levillain demonstrates in this book, echoes the topography of Merseyside – the 'terrible city' is represented by the Shell oil refinery, glowing infernally across the water, its advertising sign, minus its S, blazing out an uncompromising message: HELL.

If the city is hell, that would seem to make the rural idyll on the other side of the river – Dollarton, Wirral – heaven, or at least an earthly paradise. Gazing across at the oil refinery in 'The Forest Path to the Spring', Lowry's protagonist reflects 'And yet, my own imagination could not have dreamt anything fairer than the heaven from which we perceived this'.[17] Indeed, Lowry writes elegiacally and beautifully

---

13 In *The Collected Poetry of Malcolm Lowry*, ed. Kathleen Scherf (Vancouver: University of British Columbia Press, 1992), p. 131.
14 Malcolm Lowry, 'Through the Panama', in *Hear Us O Lord*, p. 68.
15 'Through the Panama', p. 59.
16 Malcolm Lowry, 'Present Estate of Pompeii', in *Hear Us O Lord*, p. 183.
17 Malcolm Lowry, 'The Forest Path to the Spring', in *Hear Us O Lord*, p. 258.

both of Dollarton and of the Wirral peninsula, with its views of the sea and the mountains and its 'feeling of space and emptiness'.[18] But he is too well grounded in the topography of myth (not to mention his own personal torments) not to understand that paradises are always and necessarily threatened by contamination – not just from without (the terrible city) but crucially also from *within*: it is human nature itself that threatens all Edens. In the middle of the idyllic Wirral golf course recalled in *Under the Volcano* lies Hell Bunker, where Jacques Laruelle accidentally plays 'Peeping Tom' on his best friend Geoffrey Firmin's fumbling sexual encounter with a local girl – foreshadowing his later betrayal of the Consul in his affair with the Consul's wife, Yvonne. No matter how apparently idyllic the setting, there is always already a snake in the grass; and for Lowry, there is also usually a hidden bottle, a scene which the Consul plays out tragi-comically in his own garden later in *Under the Volcano*, and which is re-echoed in the bleak short story 'Gin and Goldenrod'.

Lowry, then, brilliantly transmutes the geography of Liverpool/Wirral into a symbolic structure that recurs throughout his writing. At the same time, as many commentators have noted (and as Colin Dilnot explores further in this book), his descriptions are often almost forensically accurate, grounded in both an extraordinary memory and the accurate attention to detail characteristic of all really good writers. Place, for Lowry, is always both real and symbolic – that is, psychogeographic. It is this combination that makes his writing so rich and rewarding to read; and it also reveals his deep affinity with one of his most important literary mentors, Herman Melville. Melville's *Moby-Dick* offers a point of connection with the third main element of Lowry's topography of North West England, after Liverpool and Wirral: the Isle of Man. Towards the end of Melville's novel, the apparently minor figure of the old Manx sailor – 'the oldest mariner of all'[19] – begins to appear as a figure symbolising ancient seafaring wisdom; and throughout Lowry's writing the figure of an old Manx fisherman or boatbuilder plays a similar role, appearing as an honoured representative of an ancient culture and a seafaring way of life.

Again, Lowry is here fusing biographical fact with symbolic fiction. He and his second wife Margerie did have as a neighbour in their Dollarton retreat a Manx fisherman, Jimmy Craige, who became a close and valued friend. Lowry also drew on a childhood visit to the Isle of Man to create an extraordinarily detailed and engaging portrait of a Manx writer in his story 'Elephant and Colosseum' – given a new context in this book by Manx artist Cian Quayle. Full of Lowry's characteristic love of language and the quirks of languages, this story ends with an incantatory celebration of Manx names, creating a kind of myth of origins – and at the same time demonstrating Lowry's eternal awareness of the fundamental duality in human nature and human fate: 'But man was Quayne, and man was Quaggan, man was

---

18   Malcolm Lowry, *Under the Volcano* (London: Penguin, 1962 [1947]), p. 23.
19   Herman Melville, *Moby-Dick; or, The Whale* (London: Penguin, 1972 [1851]), p. 632.

Quillish, man was Qualtrough, man was Quirk and Quayle and Looney, and Illiam Dhone, who had been hanged. And yet lived – because he was innocent?'[20]

Establishing the terrain

In a justly famous letter written in 1946 to Jonathan Cape, making the case (successfully, as it turned out) for the publication of *Under the Volcano* complete and without the cuts suggested by Cape's reader, Lowry finished with a bold claim:

> For the book was so designed, counterdesigned and interwelded that it could be read an indefinite number of times and still not have yielded all its meanings or its drama or its poetry.[21]

The essays published in this book demonstrate, we believe, that – a century after his birth and just over fifty years after his death – Lowry's writings (perhaps especially, but not only, *Under the Volcano*) continue to prove richly inspiring sources of meanings, drama and poetry. It's also fair to say that the 'Lowrytrek' itself, Lowry's mythmaking, coincidence-ridden, accident-prone life – described by his biographer Gordon Bowker as perhaps 'his most complex and compelling fictional contrivance of all'[22] – has proved an equally fertile source of inspiration for a wide range of creative artists.

While some of the contributions to this book take the form of scholarly essays, the book is not a collection of academic writings on Lowry. Rather, the pieces take a variety of approaches – creative, literary-critical, geographical, theoretical, fictional, anecdotal – to Lowry and his work. There is a particular focus on place and on journeys; contributors write from the UK, Europe, Canada and Mexico, and reflect both on Lowry's own journeys and on their own journeys with and through Lowry's work.

Poet Ian McMillan begins with a personal story of his encounter with *Under the Volcano* – 'a story of misreading and mishearings and misunderstandings and long hours at sea and long hours on trains'. Colin Dilnot, an artist and photographer who lives on the Wirral, provides a snapshot of his fascinating and ongoing project to investigate and map the geographical contours of Lowry's early years. Moving outwards from the Wirral, Cian Quayle reflects, through text and images, on the place and meanings of the Isle of Man for Lowry. Continuing across the Atlantic, Michele Gemelos gives an intriguing reading of the Liverpool/New York dynamic, and the complexities of home, family and origins, in Lowry's novella *Lunar Caustic*; 'writing in New York', she argues, Lowry uses a distinctively 'Liverpool' literary voice 'to capture another city in similar crisis, to balance its contradictions, and to try to deal with those personal ones that he imported'. From New York we travel

---

20 Malcolm Lowry, 'Elephant and Colosseum', in *Hear Us O Lord*, p. 174.
21 Letter to Jonathan Cape, 2 January 1946, in *Selected Letters*, p. 88. This letter, which runs to 31 printed pages, is a fascinating exposition of the many layers and facets of *Under the Volcano* and shows Lowry's extraordinary talents as a letter-writer.
22 *Pursued by Furies*, p. xv.

south to Mexico, the setting and the *genius loci* of Lowry's masterwork. Alberto Rebollo, guiding spirit of the Malcolm Lowry Foundation in Cuernavaca, gives an impassioned account of Lowry as the writer who, more even than most Mexican writers, has captured the truth of Mexico – and who, beyond any considerations of place, has written a novel of 'human solidarity against death, human solidarity against isolation and the devastation of the world'.

At the centre of the book, and as it were giving a conceptual grounding to the whole, Mark Goodall gives background to the notion of 'psychogeography' and makes a convincing case both for the value of such an approach to Lowry and for Lowry's own creative process as fundamentally psychogeographic; as he points out, in his letter to Cape Lowry describes the first chapter of *Under the Volcano* as 'above all establish[ing] the *terrain*'. Mark's piece is followed by Ailsa Cox's short story, which takes up the themes, so central to *Under the Volcano*, of circulating words – letters which may or may not reach their destination, may or may not even be sent – and of the absolute necessity, above all, of love.

From the volcanic landscapes of Mexico we follow Lowry to the northern idyll of Dollarton, Canada. Annick Drösdal-Levillain shows how Lowry's Canadian 'paradise' was fundamentally imbued with the Wirral of his childhood; at the same time, she celebrates the 'echo-system' of Lowry's writing, beautifully revealing the 'treasures' his work holds for 'the reader willing to lend a "floating ear"'. Liverpool-born Nicholas Murray also focuses on Lowry's Canadian writing, in this case recounting how Lowry's last work, the unfinished *October Ferry to Gabriola*, appeared in his own life as a book he was 'destined to read'; *October Ferry*, Murray argues, is 'occasionally a flawed novel, but it is a richly rewarding and haunting one in its celebration of human freedom and the determination to find a meaningful path or embark on the redeeming voyage'. Approaching Lowry from a rather different angle, writer and musician Michael Turner tells the wonderful story of how he came to create The Malcolm Lowry Room, a Vancouver nightclub 'within mortar fire' of Lowry's Dollarton paradise, popular with bikers, playing host to the fabulous-sounding Demolition Doll Rods ('a band that performed naked but for carefully placed pieces of gaffer tape, with two of the members in the midst of gender reassignment'), and presided over by huge photos of our hero himself 'in his bathing trunks, standing guard'.

Finally, we come full circle. Writer and poet Robert Sheppard weaves together multiple times and multiple journeys to create a haunting (and haunted) depiction of his pilgrimage to Lowry's grave in Ripe, Sussex; and Gordon Bowker, author of the highly acclaimed biography of Lowry, *Pursued by Furies*, provides an overview of Lowry's life and his place in the literary pantheon; he is, Bowker argues, 'probably the most neglected genius of modern English literature'.

Edward Burra, *Skeleton Party*, c. 1952–54,
watercolour on paper support, 71.8 x 104.1 cm

© The Estate of Edward Burra, courtesy Lefevre Fine Art, London

Lowry, creative catalyst

Like that of the writer W. G. Sebald, Lowry's contemporary influence extends beyond literature to artists working across the creative spectrum. Film maker John Huston (with his adaptation of *Under the Volcano*), jazz musician Graham Collier (UK), artists Ron Bolt (Canada), Julian Cooper (UK) and Alberto Gironella (Mexico), playwright Michael Mercer (Canada) and choreographer Angus Balbernie (UK) are just some of the artists who have made work directly inspired by him. An 'Under the Volcano' festival of art and social change takes place annually in Vancouver; a contemporary art exhibition focusing on *Under the Volcano*, entitled *Quauhnahuac – Die Gerade ist eine Utopie* (*The Straight Line is a Utopia*), was presented at the Kunsthalle Basel in 2006; French performance company Cercle Pan staged a multimedia event dedicated to Lowry in 2008; songs as diverse as Jack Bruce's 'The Consul at Sunset' (with lyrics by Pete Brown) and 'Under the Volcano' by the Red Sea Sharks have been recorded; and there is even a band named Malcolm Lowry on the Berlin club scene.

Indeed this book is being published as part of a wide-ranging cultural programme taking place in Liverpool to mark Lowry's centenary. Organised by the Bluecoat, the arts centre located just round the corner from the Anatomy Museum in Paradise Street that so horrified Lowry in the 1920s, this comprises an exhibition by contemporary UK and international artists working in film, painting, photography, printmaking, drawing and installation, and, like this publication, it reflects Lowry's creative orbit. There are also specially commissioned music, performance and literature events and a film programme, tours and talks, a day-long *dérive* taking in resonant Lowry sites, and a Day of the Dead altar dedicated to Lowry. We have integrated images from the Bluecoat exhibition into this book, not just to complement and enhance the texts, but as images in their own right. In the short biographies of contributors to the book, these artists speak of Lowry's impact on their work.

'Wonders are many': Lowry's legacy

> [*Under the Volcano*] can be regarded as a kind of symphony, or in another way as a kind of opera - or even a horse opera. It is hot music, a poem, a song, a tragedy, a comedy, a farce, and so forth. It is superficial, profound, entertaining and boring, according to taste. It is a prophecy, a political warning, a cryptogram, a preposterous movie, and a writing on the wall.[23]

Just as Lowry's life and work strike a chord beyond literature with other areas of the arts, so too can we approach his work in new ways to find readings appropriate for our times. The curator of the Basel exhibition mentioned above argued that the Consul's 'existential struggle and ultimate failure become metaphors for the

---

23   Lowry, letter to Cape, 2 January 1946, *Selected Letters*, p. 66.

advance and simultaneous regression of modern man';[24] meanwhile, Lowry's environmentalism looks increasingly prescient today, as we live in the shadow of impending global environmental catastrophe. The volcano smoulders but will we heed its warning?

Reading the essays commissioned for this book as they came in, we were struck by the fact that several of the writers mentioned a particular response to Lowry's work: a powerful feeling that his writing was somehow speaking personally to them; that they were somehow *meant* to find it; or that, having found it, they seemed to know it already. This must speak to the strength, the universality and the human spirit of Lowry's writing – as well as to his extraordinary ability to put into words the particular truth of a specific place. As we hope this book demonstrates, readers continue to find in Lowry's work multiple layers of meaning, richly suggestive treatments of the fundamental dramas of human life, and the poetry of a great writer – writing that is accurate, powerful, sometimes frightening, and often extremely funny. Indeed this last characteristic is perhaps unsurprising given the particular Merseyside penchant for humour, the famous Scouse wit and quick-witted, sometimes darkly surreal, wordplay. Lowry was fond of the remark of the eighteenth-century lawyer Oliver Edwards, quoted in Boswell's *Life* of Johnson: 'I have tried too in my time to be a philosopher, but [...] cheerfulness was always breaking in'. It is, in fact, impossible to read Lowry's work, no matter how dark its themes, without feeling uplifted by his exuberant love of language, of humanity and of the world. As he wrote in his letter to Cape of *Under the Volcano*: 'when you get to the end, if you have read carefully, you should want to turn back to the beginning again, where it is not impossible, too, that your eye might alight once more upon Sophocles' *Wonders are many, and none is more wonderful than man* – just to cheer you up'.[25]

We hope that, in showcasing a wide variety of creative responses to Lowry, this book will demonstrate his ongoing significance as a writer and a thinker – a writer deeply grounded in the North West of England, yet fully deserving of the appellation 'curious internationalist'. Above all, we hope that it will encourage readers to embark on their own 'voyage that never ends' – whether outward bound for the first time, or returning, as Cian Quayle puts it in this book, 'to that which was previously known' – through the writing of Malcolm Lowry.

Bryan Biggs and Helen Tookey

Liverpool, 2009

24   Press release, 2006.
25   Letter to Cape, 2 January 1946, p. 88.

Adrian Henri, *Calaveras, The Dance (after Posada)*, 1993,
pencil on paper, 16.5 x 11.5 cm

Estate of Adrian Henri

Malcolm Lowry: who he was and who I was and who I am

Ian McMillan

This is a story of misreading and mishearings and misunderstandings and long hours at sea and long hours on trains. My dad was born in 1919 in Carnwath, a village quite near Lanark and not far from a place called Biggar. 'London's big but Biggar's Biggar', as he often said in idle moments. Maybe the idea that you could play with language began there, in a layby near the Carter Bar and the Scottish Border, one Easter when my dad said it about ten times in the space of as many minutes as he was pumping the old stove and my mother told him to stop.

My dad joined the Royal Navy in 1938 and spent twenty years at sea, retiring when I was two years old, and spending another twenty-odd years working in an office in Sheffield, leaving at the same time every morning and coming home (often with a Fat Heid, as he called a headache) at the same time every evening. He never spoke much about the sea because I think he thought it might be boring to me and my brother, but I could tell that it was in his blood, pumping through his veins in waves. He rolled as he walked, and he stood to attention beside the table when he'd had his tea. Sometimes he let something slip, about the beauty of the South China Sea in the evening or of the horror of chasing the *Bismarck* through a storm. Then he'd go and sit in the conservatory making fishing flies and singing Andy Stewart songs in a tenor voice that broke your heart. It always felt to me, as he sang and tied the flies, that he was yearning for some idealised version of home. He'd call it *hame*, of course, which broke my heart even more.

As a boy I read comics from Jack Brooks's newsagents brought by mother when she returned from her fortnightly expeditions to get her hair done. The comics were a mixed bunch over the years, anything from the *Beano* and the *Dandy* to the *Sparky* and the *Beezer* and the *Victor* and the *Valiant* and copies of a long-forgotten publication called *Classics Illustrated*; great novels transformed into brightly coloured comics. I remember reading *The Man in the Iron Mask* and *Treasure Island*, *Oliver Twist* and *The Time Machine*. I'm sorry to report that *Under the Volcano* by Malcolm Lowry wasn't a *Classics Illustrated*, but *Moby-Dick* was, it certainly was.

I'm telling you all this, about my dad at sea, and singing and tying fishing flies, about the *Classics Illustrated* edition of *Moby-Dick*, and about a yearning for home, as a way in to talking about Malcolm Lowry and *Under the Volcano* because, even though I didn't really know it at the time, it was the book I was waiting to discover as I sat at home waiting for my mam to come home with the comics and my dad to come with his *fat heid*. I don't really know if books can lie in wait for you like dogs or muggers, but it always felt like *Under the Volcano* was a book that I'd read several times even before I first picked it up. And then, the odd thing is that I picked it up and bought it and looked at it many times before I actually read it. *Perhaps because I'd read it many times before.*

Imagine the time; the mid-1970s, an era that seems very long ago in a kind of mist. Imagine the place: Stafford, about as far away from the sea as you can get. Imagine me: Ian McMillan, clever kid at school, bit of a rebel at Polytechnic, looking for someone to read for my extended essay in my third year of the Modern Studies degree that I wasn't really working very hard for. I'd enjoyed the Beat poets and Walt Whitman and Herman Melville but that was about it. I still read the Steinbeck and Hemingway that I'd read when I was in the sixth form, and I was looking for a new literary hero, someone to base my nascent sense of poetic self around, and I stumbled on Malcolm Lowry, and *Under the Volcano*.

It was the cover that attracted me to the book first, although to my shame I can't recall where I bought it. It cost 80p. The edition, in the Penguin Modern Classics published in 1975, had a detail of a fresco on the front by Diego Rivera (about whom I knew nothing at the time) called *Day of the Dead in the City* and it featured a trilbied guy in a shirt and tie glugging what looked like the end of a pint of Barnsley Bitter. He looked like I wanted to look; he looked cool and scruffy and a little bit abandoned and a little bit lost. He looked like I thought I might look halfway through one of our social nights at the Poly, where we'd been bopping to The Motors and buying whisky at 10p (a fraction of an *Under the Volcano*) from Alf the Barman whom I hilariously kept calling the Half a Barman. I suspect Malcolm Lowry might have liked that gag: nobody else did.

I was also attracted to the title: *Under the Volcano*. I had no idea what it meant. Under which volcano? Who was under the volcano? Why should you be under a volcano? Where was the volcano and what was it like to be under it? Mind you, all those thoughts were unarticulated and inchoate because what I really liked was the sound of the words and the way they rang like a bell, which would find an echo in the book, which rings with bells all the way through. I found myself saying the words Under the Volcano over and again until they stopped having any meaning but simply sounded like a set of muffled notes on a faraway drum.

So I read the book in the refectory at North Staffordshire Polytechnic and on the early train I used to get from Stafford to Manchester and from there to Barnsley at seven o'clock on a Saturday morning after the gigs. I loved the early mornings, I still do, and I was heartened almost to the point of tears to note that Geoffrey Firmin did too, and I tried to pretend, as I walked down Newport Road to Stafford Station, that I was walking to the bar called the Farolito, the little lighthouse, that only opened at four o'clock in the morning, in time for a little nip before I bought my ticket.

At first, like many people do, I struggled with the book. That first chapter is hard work for a kid from the coalfields who picked the book up on the strength of the cover. Of course I found out, like many people do, that if you persist with the book beyond chapter one, then it opens up like a flower, or rather like a drunk offering you a flower just before he stumbles and falls.

You all know the book, so I won't offer you an analysis, but there are certain paragraphs I carry round with me whole like a tattoo or a taste or the echo of a shopping list that you memorised as a child. In some ways I've never really got over that first infatuation with the sound of the title, and the book often (and I reread it once every couple of years: it would be more often, but life is short) reads to me more like a song than a novel. I couldn't care less about the plot: what I want are those marvellous singing sentences, building like clouds. How's this, from chapter two and Yvonne's first meeting with Geoffrey on her return. It's early morning and the Consul is drunk and Yvonne wants to cry. But listen to the words, listen to the words…

> 'Well, actually I've only been away once.' The Consul took a long shuddering drink, then sat down again beside her. 'To Oaxaca, – Remember Oaxaca?'
>
> ' – Oaxaca? – '
>
> ' – Oaxaca – '
>
> – The word was like a breaking heart, a sudden peal of stifled bells in a gale, the last syllables of one dying of thirst in the desert. Did she remember Oaxaca! The roses and the great tree, was that, the dust and the buses to Etla and Nochitlán? and: *'damas acompañadas de un caballero, gratis!'* Or at night their cries of love, rising into the ancient fragrant Mayan air, heard only by ghosts…

That sentence that begins 'The word was like a breaking heart…' has stayed with me for decades, and I've played it over and over again in my head until, like an old-style cassette that's almost worn away, that 'sudden peal of stifled bells in a gale' has been reduced, or expanded, or diluted, or enlarged in my head until it's become pure sound, pure memory, pure image.

So, in that final year at North Staffs Poly I read the book many times when I should have been reading about politics and history and sociology. I read a lot about Lowry and I saw links between his love of the sea and my dad's love of the sea; they both needed to escape, they both needed wider and wider horizons. My dad was a teetotaller and he didn't swear but he'd sailed to Mexico many times so for me he was almost Lowry in a kilt. I misread *Under the Volcano*, too. I misread it heroically because I was listening for the music and not for the meaning; for many years (until fairly recently, I'm ashamed to say) I thought that all the action took place in Oaxaca. I know, I know: that's ridiculous. The novel happens in Quauhnahuac, not Oaxaca, although actually it mostly happens in my head, let's face it. I got a 2:2 for my extended essay, which isn't surprising. It's as though I'd written about all the action of *Two Gentlemen of Verona* happening in Grimsby between tides.

When I left North Staffs Poly for the last time, walking to the station in the early Lowry morning sometime in 1978, I didn't have my copy of *Under the Volcano* with me. In a Lowryesque gesture I'd given it to a first-year girl called Karen who'd expressed interest in the book, again mainly because of the cover. Years later, at a writing workshop in Devon, she gave me the book back and my heart leaped when I saw it. The cover still excited me, and the words still sang. I was embarrassed by the comments I'd made in the margins, though, and the words and paragraphs I'd underlined and asterisked. I'd noted links that may have been spurious but at the time I thought they were pure Lowry. Or maybe pure McMillan. Or maybe pure McLowry. On page III I underlined something about some stamps showing 'archers shooting at the sun...' and I wrote in the margin 'See p102' and on page 102 I underlined some words about a bird that 'glided down to alight near them like a spent arrow' and I scribbled 'see pIII' in the margin. I underlined phrases and sentences with *black* or *white* in them because I thought the book was about duality, and I underlined references to time, particularly references to hours, because even in my addled brain I understood that the book revolved partly around the idea of time, and partly around the conceit of hours. Why, there's even a reference to a month called Mac. I like that month.

So, the novel stays with me for all kinds of reasons that maybe have more to do with me and the times than with Malcolm.

One more story: years later, in 1997, I went to Oaxaca at the request of the British Council; I was also making a travel film for local television and after my reading we went to a bar that I convinced myself was the Farolito. We sat and ate and drank and suddenly a man walked in with a rose. He presented it to a woman at the next table and she burst into tears. He walked out. He came back. He gave her another rose and she wept and wept. This happened a number of times and it felt to me like I was watching Geoffrey and Yvonne or Malcolm and Margerie. Eventually the man came in again with another rose, followed by an ancient woman who looked like the old lady in the Farolito. It turned out she was one of those rose sellers who haunt the streets of Mexico and she began to batter the man with her empty rose basket and a couple of coppers came in and gave him the bum's rush. The weeping woman stood up and said, 'He was the father of my child!' Up in the sky, a moon like a pound hung and hung until a cloud ushered it away.

Adrian Henri, *Calaveras for Catherine*, 1998,
drawing on green paper, 29 x 23 cm

Collection of Catherine Marcangeli

OVERLEAF: Adrian Henri, *The Day of the Dead, Hope Street*, 1998,
acrylic on canvas, 193 x 243 cm (detail)

Estate of Adrian Henri

Lowry, as the white-suited Consul, appears on the extreme left
of the painting

the Consul white suit crumpled
lounges in the doorway of the Philharmonic Pub
tequila in hand
bloodred tropical sunset
reflected in his eyes

from 'The Day of the Dead, Hope Street' by Adrian Henri

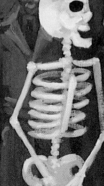

Lowry's birthplace, 13 North Drive, New Brighton, today

Photo by Colin Dilnot

Lowry's Wirral

Colin Dilnot

I had known Lowry's work since I first went to university in the 1970s. However, it was not until I moved to his birthplace, New Brighton on the Wirral peninsula, in the mid-1980s that I began to take an active interest in the topography of his life and work. Although considerable research has been undertaken on Lowry's early life, there still exist inaccuracies in published biographical accounts. As we approach the centenary of his birth, I have been trying to address some of these inaccuracies and to unearth further information on Lowry's Wirral, where his family home remained after he left England, and to which he never returned. My research to date has involved detailed readings of his work to identify how far his descriptions match Wirral locales; placing the locations he describes in a historical context; and trying to glean further information from his manuscripts and other papers, held principally by the University of British Columbia in Vancouver. This essay can only give a flavour of my research so far.

Lowry's birthplace: 13 North Drive

Writings on Lowry include a range of suggestions relating to his birthplace, including these by Douglas Day, Muriel Bradbrook and Gordon Bowker:

> The subject of these obsequies was born Clarence Malcolm Lowry, on July 28, 1909, at 'Warren Crest,' North Drive, Liscard (now incorporated into the township of Wallasey), in the Birkenhead district of Cheshire, England.[1]

> Mr and Mrs Lowry, starting in New Brighton close to the Methodist church, moved in 1906 to a relatively modest but substantial villa, where Malcolm was born. It stands on the very highest point of the red sandstone ridge overlooking fifteen golf courses, four light-houses, the sand-dunes and market gardens of the Wirral Peninsula.[2]

> On Thursday 29th July, the births columns in the *Liverpool Echo* announced: '*LOWRY* – July 28th, at Warren Crest, North-drive, New Brighton, to Mr and Mrs Arthur Lowry, a son'.[3]

In his essay 'Paradise Street Blues', Chris Ackerley draws on the above descriptions but goes on to say: 'The house is no longer there, Wallasey having suffered heavy bomb damage during the Second World War and the site redeveloped'.[4]

---

1   Douglas Day, *Malcolm Lowry: A Biography* (New York: Oxford University Press, 1973), p. 54.
2   Muriel Bradbrook, *Malcolm Lowry: His Art and Early Life: A Study in Transformation* (Cambridge: Cambridge University Press, 1974), p. 29
3   Gordon Bowker, *Pursued by Furies: A Life of Malcolm Lowry* (London: Harper Collins, 1993), p. 7.
4   Chris Ackerley, 'Paradise Street Blues: Malcolm Lowry's Liverpool', in Michael Murphy and Deryn Rees-Jones (eds.), *Writing Liverpool: Essays and Interviews* (Liverpool: Liverpool University Press, 2007), p. 56.

Ackerley bases this assertion on an article by Lowry's brother, Russell, published in the *Malcolm Lowry Review* in 1987 in response to a piece by Mark Thomas, titled 'Pilgrimage to Caldy', in the same journal: 'Warren Crest wasn't worth looking for. It isn't there any more. Wallasey suffered heavy bomb damage during WW2. I understand the site has been redeveloped.'[5] Because of the nearness of Liverpool, and Lowry's association with the city, some commentators have also given Liverpool as Lowry's birthplace.

If we look at the history of Lowry's birthplace, this confusion among different commentators is understandable. In 1909, for instance, North Drive was in New Brighton, which was part of the County Borough of Wallasey. The electoral ward of New Brighton and later Warren (New Brighton was split into several voting wards as the town grew) was in the Parish of Liscard. When Lowry was born, Wallasey was in the County of Cheshire; but in 1974 it was amalgamated, along with other districts – including Birkenhead – into the Metropolitan Borough of Wirral.

I went to North Drive armed with Bowker's information and Bradbrook's descriptions, assuming that the house must have been on the cliff side of the road. When I couldn't find a Warren Crest I supposed that it had long gone. I consulted the Ordnance Survey map for 1909, saw that there were three large houses on the cliff side and assumed that one of those must have been Warren Crest.

I then visited the local reference library and discovered that the electoral register for 1909 and 1911 had Lowry's father Arthur living at No. 13, on the opposite side of the road, with no mention of Warren Crest. The 1911 *Gore's Directory* confirmed that Arthur Lowry was living at No. 13 and additionally showed that the property was called Warren Crest – which to date is the only documentary evidence of this, other than the birth record in the *Liverpool Echo* and Russell Lowry's statements.

But what of Russell Lowry's belief that Warren Crest 'isn't there any more'? I went back to the library and confirmed the following:

- The odd numbers in the road have not changed from 1909 until today.

- The 1909 OS map shows three houses on the cliff side of the road. I have now identified the names of these houses as Lingcroft, Tigh-na-Mara and Oriente. I have also identified who occupied them from 1909 through to 1920, and the Lowrys are not included. The map shows that there was a gap between what I believe was Tigh-na-Mara and Lingcroft, which would have given the Lowrys (at No. 13) a view of the sea which is not apparent today. This demonstrates that it is not a gap caused by bombing.

- A further house appears on the 1935 OS map next to Lingcroft, which is No. 6 North Drive. At some point, the houses were numbered 2/4/6/8 and

---

5   Russell Lowry, 'Clearing Up Some Problems', *Malcolm Lowry Review*, 21 and 22 (Fall 1987 and Spring 1988), pp. 100-102.

this is still the case today, except that on the site of No. 2 (Oriente?) there is a block of flats called Compass Court, built in the 1970s/80s. A further modern house has been built in the last ten years in the remaining 1909 gap between No. 4 and No. 6, blocking the sea view.

- A Heywoods family occupied No. 13 in 1939 and were still there in 1945, 1946 and 1947, so the house does not appear to have been destroyed/damaged in the war and subsequently rebuilt/repaired.

- An OS map in the library shows every bomb dropped on Wallasey. There does not appear to have been any war damage in North Drive. The Wallasey Historical Society published a book on Wallasey's war years and there is no mention of bombs dropping in North Drive. The OS map also shows that the nearest bombs to 13 North Drive were both over 100 yards away with many houses in between, including the large house (No. 8) across the road from No. 13. No. 8 is still standing and does not appear to have been rebuilt. Although this is not definitive proof that Warren Crest was not damaged, I cannot believe that either bomb was powerful enough to have caused the total destruction of the property. That would have meant that many other houses in the area would have been reduced to rubble as well, and that was not the case.

What we have in the electoral register is constant and consistent proof of the Lowry family living at No. 13 North Drive, plus a picture of the other dwellings in the road, which supports the location of Malcolm's birthplace and the fact that it is still standing intact.

Braeside Preparatory School

Both Douglas Day and Gordon Bowker have documented in their respective biographies of Lowry that he attended the Braeside Preparatory School between 1914 and 1916. Both biographers offer scant information about Lowry's first school. Various internet searches turned up a lead that the school used to be located in Kirby Park, West Kirby, which is under a mile from Lowry's second home, Inglewood in Caldy. A search of the 1891 and 1901 censuses confirmed that the school was in Kirby Park but gave no precise address. At the time, Kirby Park was the name of the southern area of West Kirby, with its own railway station on the West Kirby to Hooton line. Kirby Park today is one road in the south of West Kirby containing many large houses, all of which represented possible candidates for a preparatory school; but there was no evidence as to which house could be Braeside.

I decided to knock on a few doors and see whether any local people had any knowledge of the school. I struck lucky with my first call, finding a woman who had lived in the area for many years and who took me to the right house. At some point in the 1900s, or perhaps earlier, the road the school was in was renamed Devonshire Road, which accounted for my inability to find the school in Kirby Park.

29

Top and middle: Braeside in West Kirby where Lowry went to school, today
Bottom: the Taskersons' home in Meols Drive, today

Photos by Colin Dilnot

The school occupied two sets of semi-detached Victorian houses numbered 17, 19, 21 and 23, with a playing field across the road, which still exists and is now a play area for local children. My guide took me to meet the current occupant of No. 19, whose house bears the nameplate 'Braeside'. She informed me that she had found graffiti carved into woodwork on the stairs from the building's time as a school, which closed before the Second World War.

In the Cheshire Records Office I discovered a 1901 trade journal, *Porter's Directory for West Kirby, Hoylake, Heswall etc*, which contained an advert for the Braeside Preparatory School giving details of the school's curriculum and philosophy:

> The Rev. A.G. Cox (late scholar of Hertford College, Oxford and Assistant Master of Bromsgrove and Birkenhead Schools) receives boys from 7 to 15 years age to prepare them for the Public Schools.

> Both at Bromsgrove (for 2.5 years) and at Birkenhead (for 9 years), Mr Cox acted in the capacity of House Master in the School House, and had special opportunities for becoming thoroughly acquainted with the internal management and discipline of a Boarding School.

> The School Course includes instruction in Latin, Greek, French, Mathematics (German, Music, Singing and Drawing, if required), together with a general knowledge of the Bible. It is Mr Cox's aim to maintain a high moral as well as intellectual standard. He feels that the development of character must necessarily be largely guided by the influences brought to bear upon a young boy at school, and he endeavours to pay as much attention to each individual out of school hours as well as the classroom. He hopes the boys entrusted to him will be prepared in every way for the wider life of the Public Schools.

> Mr Cox has the assistance of Resident Masters for French and Mathematics, and of Music and Singing Teachers, and Drill Sergeant.

> The domestic arrangements are in the hands of a Lady Matron, who does everything to secure the comfort and health of the boys.

> A Prospectus of the School will be supplied on application to the Head Master.

> The House stands in a very healthy position; there is a Carpenter's Shop and an excellent Gymnasium attached to the School as well as a field for cricket and football, commanding a full view of the mountains and the sea.

Not only do we get a flavour of the school day for Malcolm but also perhaps an indication of why Arthur Lowry sent his sons Malcolm and Russell to the school: Mr Cox's aim 'to maintain a high moral as well as intellectual standard' must have appealed to Arthur's Wesleyan philosophy as much as the short distance his sons had to travel. The availability of a sports field and gymnasium must also have appealed to the health-conscious Arthur.

The Taskersons' house

The Taskerson family are characters in Lowry's *Under the Volcano*. They 'adopt' Geoffrey Firmin, the novel's hero, as a boy. It is while on holiday in France with the Taskersons that Geoffrey meets Jacques Laruelle, whose reminiscences of his friend a year after his death open the novel. After the holiday meeting, Laruelle is invited to visit the Taskersons' home in Leasowe, England.

According to Russell Lowry, his brother based the Taskersons on a local Wirral family, the Furnisses. In his preface to Ann Smith's book *The Art of Malcolm Lowry* Russell points out the attraction the family had for Malcolm:

> A big quiet room at the top of the house [Inglewood] was furnished as a study for him. No good. No booze. No amusing company. He seems to have found both among the Furness [Russell's spelling] brothers – later sublimated into the Taskersons. Malcolm had known them at his first school, years earlier. I never met them. With the Furness brothers Malcolm did his marathon beerwalks and of course found Inglewood even more boring when he got back.[6]

With the aid of Russell's memoir, Gordon Bowker established that the Furniss family had lived at Clevelands in Meols Drive, West Kirby during the time that Lowry knew them.[7] Lowry had originally met James Furniss at Braeside, where James rescued him from being bullied. Lowry gives us the following description of the Taskersons' home in the first chapter of *Under the Volcano*:

> The Taskersons lived in a comfortable house whose back garden abutted on a beautiful, undulating golf course abounded on the far side by the sea. It looked like the sea; actually it was the estuary, seven miles wide, of a river: white horses westward marked where the real sea began. The Welsh mountains gaunt and black and cloudy, with occasionally a snow peak to remind Geoff of India, lay across the river. During the week, when they were allowed to play, the course was deserted: yellow ragged sea poppies fluttered in the spiny sea grass. On the shore were the remains of an antediluvian forest with ugly black stumps showing, and farther up an old stubby deserted lighthouse. There was an island in the estuary, with a windmill on it like a curious black flower, which you could ride out to at low tide on a donkey. The smoke of freighters outward bound from Liverpool hung low on the horizon. There was a feeling of space and emptiness. Only at week-ends did a certain disadvantage appear in their site: although the season was drawing to a close and the grey hydropathic hotels on the promenades were emptying, the golf course was packed all day with Liverpool brokers playing foursomes.[8]

---

6   Russell Lowry, 'Preface', in Ann Smith (ed.), *The Art of Malcolm Lowry* (New York: Harper and Row, 1978), p. 22.
7   Bowker, *Pursued by Furies*, p. 27.
8   Malcolm Lowry, *Under the Volcano* (Harmondsworth: Penguin, 1963 [1947]), p. 23.

The Submerged Forest Meols looking towards Hoylake

Top: Royal Liverpool Golf Course clubhouse
Middle: Hilbre Island. Bottom: Submerged forest, Meols

I was interested in finding out whether Clevelands still existed and, if it did, then how it fitted into the topography of *Under the Volcano*. An internet search revealed that a house called Clevelands still existed on Meols Drive at No. 103, now split into three flats. I spoke to one of the residents who told me that the house had always been called Clevelands. A check of the 1911 Census showed that at that time John and Mary Furniss and their family lived at 2 Grosvenor Road in West Kirby. However, the 1920 Electoral Register confirmed that the family had by then moved to 103 Meols Drive.

The importance of confirming the exact location of the Furniss home is that we can now revisit the topography of *Under the Volcano* and compare Lowry's descriptions to the actual location. George Woodcock was one the earliest commentators on Lowry's use of place in his novels. His essay 'The Own Place of the Mind' in Ann Smith's *The Art of Malcolm Lowry* demonstrates that Lowry's landscapes are based on real places. Over the years, other commentators have discussed the topography of 'Leasowe'. Muriel Bradbrook states:

> To stand at the site of either of the Lowrys' homes is to look westwards over a wide scene of great beauty and variety. Behind, and eastward, across the Mersey estuary, lies the port of Liverpool, which for Lowry came to symbolise hell; before, the expanse of the Bay. Green levels behind the dunes stretch towards the Clwyd range; the sunsets are of extraordinary brilliance. This was Lowry's first Eden.
>
> The topography of Leasowe lighthouse, the sunken remains of the primeval forest in the early golfing scenes of *Under the Volcano* are all faithful, though the scene is not placed on those links where Lowry played.[9]

In his biography, Bowker affirms Bradbrook's descriptions of Leasowe. Chris Ackerley suggests that Bradbrook and Bowker 'both fail to account for the "geography of the imagination", or degree to which [Lowry] re-arranged and mythologized the landscape'. Ackerley suggests that Lowry

> moved his Caldy home to Leasowe (between Hoylake and New Brighton), to get the view (bay, freighters, sunken forest and lighthouse), but has retained the setting of the Royal Liverpool Links at Hoylake (the island to which one might ride is Hilbre, accessible from West Kirby at low tide). Moreover, the details are more than 'precisely observed': the 'antediluvian' forest intimates the novel's Atlantis theme; the lighthouse, the Farolito; the windmill, Don Quixote; and the 'black flower', a song called 'Flores negras' sung in the *Salón Ofélia*.[10]

---

9   Bradbrook, *Malcolm Lowry*, p. 30.
10   Ackerley, 'Paradise Street Blues', p. 57.

Ackerley goes on to cast doubt on the location of Hell Bunker, where Laruelle accidentally 'play[s] Peeping Tom' on Geoffrey and his girl (*Under the Volcano*, p. 27), although both Russell Lowry and Bradbrook contend that Lowry was referring to the eighth hole on the Royal Liverpool golf course.[11]

Let us examine the location in more detail.

- Leasowe is a real place, lying – as described by Ackerley – between Hoylake and New Brighton. However, if we look at the actual topography described by Lowry, it fits the Hoylake surroundings of Clevelands better than Leasowe. Lowry may have preferred the Old English name, derived from *lea*, a meadow land – in effect the Wallasey Meadows.

- The lighthouse is an enduring image in Lowry's work. The real-life lighthouse most commentators refer to is the one at Leasowe, for obvious reasons. However, up to the early twentieth century Hoylake had two lighthouses, the Lower and Upper Lights. The Upper Light still exists; the Lower Light was demolished in 1932. Lowry's description of an 'old stubby deserted lighthouse' matches these lighthouses rather than the more conventionally shaped one at Leasowe.

- The Lower Light fell into disuse in 1908 and the grounds around the lighthouse became home to concert parties, pierrot shows and reviews. New buildings were added and, in 1920, the Pavilion Cinema opened, with an entrance through the lighthouse. Though it is not documented anywhere, Lowry must have known about or attended the cinema because Russell stated that he and Malcolm frequented all the cinemas in the local area, including Hoylake.[12] In *Under the Volcano*, Laruelle remembers that he and Geoffrey, at Leasowe, would 'walk through the sunlit windy streets or [...] look at one of the comical Pierrot shows on the beach' (pp. 23–24).

- The golf course mentioned by Lowry has to be the Royal Liverpool. The links are directly opposite Clevelands across Meols Drive, though not 'abutting' the back garden. Lowry refers to Laruelle crossing the eighth fairway to get to Leasowe (Meols)

---

11 Ackerley writes: 'According to Bradbrook, this bunker was "a well-known hazard" of the eighth hole (a short par 5) of the Royal Liverpool Links in Hoylake. Russell Lowry confirms this, adding that it was filled in before the Second World War, but I am not convinced, for when I visited Hoylake nobody at the club could recall the name. The name was probably transposed from the fourteenth hole of the Old Course at St Andrews, a long par 5 with a huge bunker left of the green'; 'Paradise Street Blues', pp. 57–58. He is quoting Bradbrook, *Malcolm Lowry*, p. 153, and Russell Lowry, 'Clearing Up Some Problems', pp. 100–102.

12 'Preface', in Smith (ed.), *The Art of Malcolm Lowry*, p. 18.

Drive and hence back to the Taskersons' (p. 27). There is still a public footpath from the shore to Meols Drive across fairways where the course dog-legs. You then come onto Meols Drive a short distance from Clevelands. Lowry describes Hell Bunker as 'a dreaded hazard, fairly near the Taskersons' house, in the middle of the long sloping eighth fairway' (p. 26). You cannot see the hole from Meols Drive by Clevelands, but if you look at the map it becomes apparent that the hole is almost directly opposite Clevelands.

- In relation to the 'hydropathic hotels' mentioned by Lowry (p. 23), there was a large hotel of this name on the West Kirby promenade only a few hundred metres from Clevelands. The hotel was located opposite to the Marine Lake in West Kirby, also mentioned by Lowry as the place where Geoffrey and Laruelle go sailing (p. 24).

I would contend that Lowry was placing his paradise around Clevelands and not 'mov[ing] his home [Inglewood] from Caldy to Leasowe', as suggested by Ackerley. The rest of the landscape then falls into place – the estuary, Hilbre Island, the submerged forest between Hoylake and Meols, the views of the Clwyd range.

We are left with a couple of Lowryean references which have escaped detection to date. Hilbre did not have a windmill, though Caldy Hill did have one, which was used by sailors as a navigation aid in the 1800s before it was destroyed. Lowry mentions many Wirral pubs in his work; some are real, for instance the Coach and Horses in Greasby in the short story 'Enter One in Sumptuous Armour',[13] but The Case is Altered (from which Geoffrey and Laruelle are thrown out after the Hell Bunker incident) appears to be a Lowryean joke. His love of Elizabethan and Jacobean theatre may explain why he used the title of Ben Jonson's play; or perhaps he did come across a pub with that name and added it to the wealth of allusions in *Under the Volcano*. I did stumble on one coincidence concerning a pub in Hoylake called The Lighthouse Inn, which was near to the Kingsway Cinema in Hoylake, frequented by the Lowry brothers. Surely, Lowry had this – among other things – in mind when he called the cantina in which Geoffrey Firmin dies 'the Farolito'?

13   Margerie Lowry (ed.), 'Enter One in Sumptuous Armour', in *Malcolm Lowry: Psalms and Songs* (New York: New American Library, 1975), pp. 232–33.

Edward Burra, *Mexican Church*, c. 1938,
gouache and ink wash on paper, 132.1 x 103.5 cm

WESTERN UNION
(THE WESTERN UNION TELEGRAPH COMPANY)
CABLEGRAM
ANGLO-AMERICAN TELEGRAPH Co., Ld.   CANADIAN NATIONAL TELEGRAPHS.

RECEIVED AT YORKSHIRE HOUSE, CHAPEL STREET, LIVERPOOL, 3. (Tel. No. Central, 2274.)

1938 MAY 12 A 4 37

2VA AB 264 MEXICOCITY 28 11

NLT AYRCLIFF   91   AYRTON AND ALDERSON SMITH
     LPL   10 DALE ST.

                                                    EPILEPSY
BRITISH CONSUL STATES LOWRY ACEPULCO SUFFERING FROM ~~EPILEPSY~~ AND ALCOHOL

UNDERSTAND OWES THOUSAND PESOS THEREFORE CANNOT LEAVE WANTS TO GO

SANDIEGO CALIFORNIA PLEASE INSTRUCT

                            LEYHAM

CABLEGRAM
ANGLO-AMERICAN TELEGRAPH Co., Ld.   CANADIAN NATIONAL TELEGRAPHS.

RECEIVED AT YORKSHIRE HOUSE, CHAPEL STREET, LIVERPOOL, 3. (Tel. No. Central, 2274).

2VA WJS L1220   1938 MAY 18 A 3

       MEXICOCITY 56 1/39 17TH

NLT AYRCLIFF   81   AYRTON & ALDERSON SMITH.
                          10 DALE ST.
     LPOOL

LOWRY REACHED MEXICOCITY HAVING PAID MOST ACAPULCO BILLS WITH

MAY ALLOWANCE NOW WISHES REMAIN HERE IS WITHOUT FUNDS AND

PRESENTABLE CLOTHING OWES APPROXIMATELY SEVEN HUNDRED PESOS

REQUESTS ABOUT SEVEN HUNDRED ADDITIONAL FOR CLOTHES SUSTENANCE

YOUR REMITTANCE

WESTERN UNION
(THE WESTERN UNION TELEGRAPH COMPANY)
CABLEGRAM

ANGLO-AMERICAN TELEGRAPH Co., Ld.   CANADIAN NATIONAL TELEGRAPHS.

RECEIVED AT YORKSHIRE HOUSE, CHAPEL STREET, LIVERPOOL, 3. (Tel. No. Central, 2274).

BLY 343 MEXICOCITY 42 15

1938 JUL 16 A 4 32 ᵍ

NLT AYRCLIFF   93   AYRTON AND ALDERSON SMITH
                              10 DALE ST.

    LPL

LOWRY PLANS LEAVE MEXICOCITY FOR LOSANGELES WEDNESDAY JULY TWENTIETH

PREVIOUS REMITTANCES EXHAUSTED SUGGEST YOU CABLE ONE HUNDRED DOLLARS

FOR TRANSPORTATION AND EXPENSES AND SUCH ADDITIONAL SUM AS FATHER

DESIRES SON TO HAVE ON PERSON WHEN ARRIVES AT DESTINATION

                    LEYHAM

Cables   U.S.A.

Cablegram

F7, EXCHANGE BUILDINGS,
LIVERPOOL, (2).

11-49

ER.1.LY564 MEXICOCITY MEX 34 26TH

    NLT AYRCLIFF LIVERPOOL.

LIVERPOOL
26 JUL
CENTRAL 0432

LOWRY LEFT MEXICOCITY JULY TWENTYTHIRD ARRIVES LOSANGELES

MORNING JULY TWENTYSEVENTH MAIL ADDRESS CARE AMERICAN

EXPRESS COMPANY INC THAT CITY WIFES ADDRESS ELEVEN THIRTY

FIVE ONE HALF LARRABEE STREET HOLLYWOOD CALIFORNIA

                    LEYHAM

Lowry with Jimmy Craige at Dollarton
University of British Columbia Library, Rare Books and Special Collections, Malcolm Lowry Collection PIOIOI53

Elliptical journeys: Malcolm Lowry, exile and return

Cian Quayle

> Who was he? Who was anybody? [...] man was Quayne, and man was
> Quaggan, man was Quillish, man was Qualtrough, man was Quirk and
> Quayle and Looney, and Illiam Dhone, who had been hanged. And yet lived
> – because he was innocent?

Malcolm Lowry, 'Elephant and Colosseum'

A photograph from the summer of 1910 shows the Lowry family on holiday in
the Isle of Man. Malcolm Lowry – barely one year old – is held by his nursemaid
Miss Bell (known as Bey) and is pictured with his father and brothers set against
a nondescript background which might be a beach – it's impossible to tell. Lowry
retained a fondness for the Isle of Man in adult life and his later stories are
permeated with references to the island. Bey, in an affectionate letter to the three-
year-old Lowry, anticipates his subsequent obsession with the sea (Lowry's mother
was the daughter of a Liverpool sea captain) and recalls how she had been seasick
on the Tynwald ferry journey to the island.

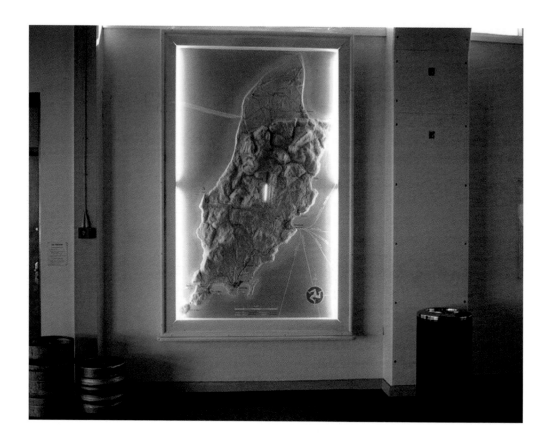

Between 1946 and 1956 Lowry worked on a series of extended short stories, which were assembled as *Hear Us O Lord from Heaven Thy Dwelling Place*. This title is also that of the Manx fishermen's hymn, which was familiar to Lowry as a Wesleyan hymn sung at his Wesleyan school. This was one of many hymns that Lowry was fascinated with and collected in his early years, in the same way that he absorbed the details and nuances of places visited, remembered and imagined. Of the stories in the collection, 'Elephant and Colosseum' is one of the longest and was regarded by Lowry as among his best work, although possibly its Manx references would make it less easily accessible to a wide audience. Its protagonist, Kennish Drumgold Cosnahan, is a Manx writer, lost and alone in Rome where he is supposed to be visiting his publisher (whose name and address he has forgotten) but actually ends up reunited, visiting the zoo, with Rosemary, the elephant he had tended on a tramp steamer's return voyage to Britain from Bangkok in 1927. As in Lowry's other works, the reader is pulled back and forth in space and time – a manifestation of Lowry's reflexive writing process, whereby family, friends and acquaintances are absorbed into a continuum which looks ahead and back as part of an elliptical journey in which he is submerged and resurfaces as the principal protagonist. The journey is constituted by the (uncompleted) cycle of novels which Lowry conceived and entitled the *The Voyage that Never Ends*.

The voyage as part of a self-imposed exile is a key feature of Lowry's life and work, beginning with his early desire to go to sea and his first voyage, in 1927, aboard the *Pyrrhus*. It was this experience which informed the writing of his first novel *Ultramarine*, and which is reflected in Cosnahan's remembered voyage in 'Elephant and Colosseum'. The sea as metaphor as well as constant physical presence –

whether the shoreline of the Wirral peninsula or the Pier Head at Liverpool, the Mersey leading out into the Irish Sea to the Isle of Man and beyond, or Lowry's Dollarton shack overlooking Burrard Inlet on the Pacific coast near Vancouver – is part of a love affair with all that is maritime. It may well have been that the 'sound' that Lowry wanted to reverberate across these stories was indeed that of the sea.

The port of Liverpool has long-established links with the Isle of Man, having served as the gateway to the rest of the world not only for seafarers, but also for tourists between the island and mainland Britain. Historically the ships of the Isle of Man Steam Packet Company were crewed by Manxmen, with stewards from Liverpool, who were known colloquially as 'boat-las'. The first port of call in the city might have been the Legs of Man coaching house on London Road, or the tattoo parlour Sailor Jack's in Tuebrook, where many people have been tattooed with the three legs or triskeles – a fertility symbol adopted by the island which finds its origin in Ancient Greece and is thought to have arrived in the Isle of Man via Sicily. Peter Heywood, midshipman on the *Bounty* and a Manxman in origin, was tattooed with the three-legs symbol after landing in Tahiti, having been set adrift in a launch with Captain Bligh (who had also lived in the Isle of Man) and others loyal to Bligh. Heywood later recounted, in a letter to his sister: 'I was tattooed not at my own desire, but theirs, for it was my constant endeavour to acquiesce in any little custom which I thought would be agreeable to them [...] I always made it a maxim when I was in Rome to act as Rome did provided it did not interfere with my morals or religion.' The mutineers, meanwhile, led by Fletcher Christian – another Manxman – settled on Pitcairn.

44

Stone-carved three legs fertility symbol at Villa Giulia, Palermo.

Arriving in Dollarton, the Lowrys were first met and befriended by Jimmy Craige and his wife. Craige, a Manxman in his sixties, had apprenticed in the Isle of Man as a boatbuilder. The Craiges formed an enduring friendship with the Lowrys, who looked after their shoreline shack whenever they were away. Craige appears as Quaggan in 'The Forest Path to the Spring', the last story in *Hear Us O Lord*, a fictionalised account of Lowry's time in Dollarton. In his biography of Lowry Gordon Bowker remarks in passing that Craige was 'married to a half-gypsy descendant of Fletcher Christian'.[1] I looked in the Isle of Man telephone directory and found six entries for the name Craige. I wrote to each one and had a return phone call from a John Craige who, in a strong Manx accent, recalled his father telling how a family member had emigrated to Canada and married a 'squaw'. Could this be the 'descendant' mentioned by Bowker, or yet another of the exaggerations and myths that surround Lowry's life and writing?

---

1   Gordon Bowker, *Pursued by Furies: A Life of Malcolm Lowry* (London: HarperCollins, 1993), p. 307.

MALCOLM LOWRY: FROM THE MERSEY TO THE WORLD

Each time Lowry settled, he returned to that which was previously known. In the hallucinatory narrative which imbues 'Elephant and Colosseum', the protagonist Cosnahan contemplates his reception at home, from afar, as he sits in a café in Rome regarding his own photograph on the dustjacket of his novel: 'Cosnahan searched the face in the photograph. He was disconcerted by the sense of difference, of no longer looking altogether at his own likeness. Yet what was unlikely was the way those eyes looked back at him.'[2]

> As we are forgiving to those who are committing trespasses us against, said the Manx. Assuming that there they were, those enemies, and, right at that moment Cosnahan looking away from his table and down the Via Veneto again, up which a huge new Cadillac the size of a conservatory was advancing soundlessly, should they recall all the beautiful old cobbled streets and ancient houses of Douglas that were still being destroyed or pulled down, and beautiful St Mathew's pulled down and the countryside ruined to make a Liverpool holiday. Yet perhaps this assumption was the great fault of the Manx. And his great fault too. The entire population of the Isle of Man seemed to be trespassing against him, for one thing, because nobody recognized him at home now that he'd become so successful in America. By which he didn't mean merely on the plane of the Browsing Manxwoman. He hadn't even seen a familiar face in Douglas, unless you counted Illiam Dhône, a man, it was true, so unique now he thought of it he might be considered a civic welcome in himself.

> For Illiam Dhône had been hanged half an age ago on a plot of ground where St Barnabas' Church now stood, and by a freak turn of fortune's wheel, survived this unpleasant ordeal.

> Later he had been pardoned, and later still proved innocent, which naturally was considered reason enough for his having survived, and this more than Lazarus of a man he'd met outside Derby Castle and they went into the pub and drank a pint of Castletown Manx oyster stout together. But so long had Cosnahan been a stranger to the old ways and the old speech that – standing under the familiar sign *Castletown 1st Prize Ales* and regarding over the bar one of these Manx calendars of singular composition for the previous November that said 24th, Last Norse King of Man died 1205, 27th, Nobles Hospital opened 1906, 30th, Winston Churchill born 1874 – he had all but forgotten that Illiam Dhône was not his companion's real name, that it was a nickname meaning sandy or fair-haired, to which the companion himself, now bald, gave no clue; all but forgotten too that this nickname wasn't strictly his own but derived, with the quirky sardonic humour of the Manx, from that other Illiam Dhôan, their own monarch martyr and rebel hero, once collogued into

---

2   Malcolm Lowry, 'Elephant and Colosseum', in *Hear Us O Lord from Heaven Thy Dwelling Place & Lunar Caustic* (London: Picador, 1991), p. 117.

47

cruel death, in fact, which no Manxman ever really forgets, shot, successfully, before his pardon arrived, Illiam Dhôan who was forefather of that famous navigator and mutineer of the H.M.S. *Bounty*, that later founder of another remoter Isle of Man, Pitcairn, and the bearer too of the great and simple name of Christian. But no relative at all of the only fellow in Europe who'd recognized Cosnahan on his first trip home in twenty years, and even this Illiam Dhône, who was an engineer's artificer and whose hands were covered with pitch, had not congratulated him, and he had been of two minds, under the circumstances, whether to congratulate Illiam Dhône.

Though in fact the latter (who had doubtless not read the Browsing Manxwoman) *had* paid him a sort of back-handed compliment:

> 'I heard roundabout, Cosnahan, you know, you had been doing quite good work.'

And Cosnahan had also thought of also saying to him:

> 'Good work, Illiam Dhône – '

So true it was that these dreamed-of moments of recognition never come off, back from the wars, back from sea, famous or in disgrace, the reception at your source was always the same; there was none – (pp. 131–32)

'Elephant and Colosseum' introduces Manx family names, place names, myths and folklore, and aspects of history that find their origin in the Isle of Man, in a merging of fact and fiction. Since Lowry did not know the island as an adult, his knowledge must have been largely distilled from his friendship and conversations with Jimmy Craige. Craige spelt with an 'e' is derived from Craig of Scotland, a name which arrived in the island via Northern Ireland. 'Kennish he believes to be a more autochthonous Manx name than his surname, though not, he says as indigenous as Quayne, Quaggan, Quillish, Qualtrough, Quale or Looney' (p. 119). Lowry made great and humorous play of the alliteration of these family names, which call out from the pages of his story.

In 2003 I exhibited *Return Ticket*, an installation of twenty photographs, each six by eight feet, along the boundary wall of the Derby Castle Depot in Douglas, Isle of Man. The images which comprise this series were drawn from an ongoing project entitled *Inventory for a Reverse Journey*. As a proposition these works trace an interweaving of time and space measured via the recollection of place at a distance.

A journey around Douglas alights at what could loosely be described as a series of landmarks, which in one form or another are reconfigured in a condensation of time, place and memory. These include the boundary walls which striate the town; a sea wall hidden behind the main street of shops, which butt up against the rear of promenade hotels; a shelter by the side of the road on the headland above a derelict holiday camp; a disused amphitheatre which hosted pierrot performances in the Victorian era; promenade shelters; and glens and gardens scattered around

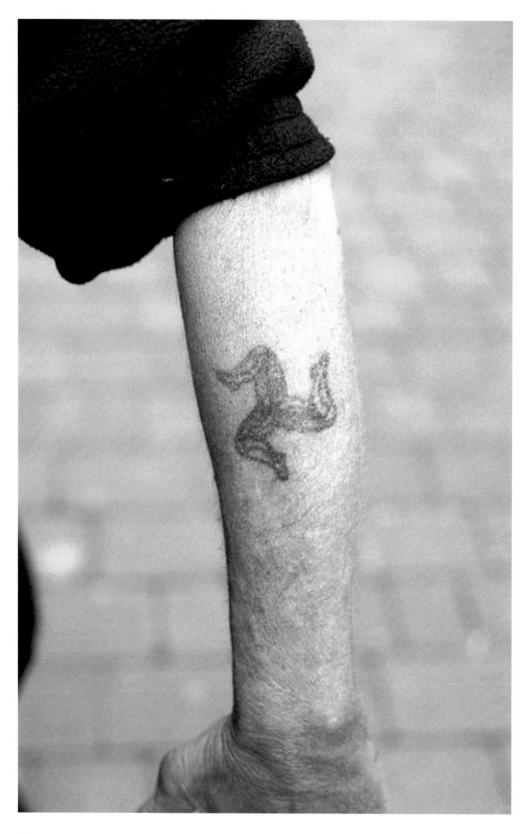

the town, which is made up of Georgian and Victorian houses often arranged in squares. One of these squares, surrounded by terraced houses, served as the site of Hutchinson 'P' Camp during the Second World War, where Kurt Schwitters, the great Dada artist (and founder of Merz, his own brand of Dada), was interned alongside other German nationals and Jewish émigrés and refugees.

In 'Elephant and Colosseum' Lowry's Cosnahan takes the reader on a journey around Douglas and its various landmarks. Each of these places bears the trace of a previous era as it has been transformed across time. This townscape grew out of the industrial era and the rise in tourism, which itself arose from lives lived through farming and fishing. The townscape of Douglas began to change, which Lowry places at the hands of a 'Liverpool holiday' but actually was radically reshaped as a

result of the island's finance-based economy and status as a tax haven, for better or worse, from the 1970s onwards. (From the early eighteenth century onwards, the island had been known for smuggling.)

Identification with a place is measured and shaded by distance. Processes of memory, myth, fact and fiction merge and are interwoven around an event or narrative which is the beginning of a journey. The Isle of Man is where I was born and grew up. A series of photographs I made in 1984 for a school geography project formed the basis of an ongoing photographic work whereby the material variants of the medium are reconfigured in a personal archive. The inventory includes family snapshots, found photographs, photographic postcards and my own photographs of the same place at different points in time. Mikhail Bakhtin, the Russian critic, proposed a form of writing which operated like a whirlpool – drawing in the world around it. In his formulation the chronotope – a definite concrete reality or locality – is subject to a transformation whereby space and time are merged in an inseparable unity, and plot and characters are unfolded within it rather than admitted to it from outside. Lowry's writing utilises a chronotopic structure whereby 'spatial and temporal indicators fuse into one carefully thought out whole. Time as it were, thickens, takes on flesh, becomes artistically visible; likewise space becomes charged and responsive to the movements of time, plot and history.'[3]

3   Mikhail Bakhtin, 'Forms of Time and of the Chronotope in the Novel', in *The Dialogic Imagination – Four Essays* (Austin: University of Texas Press, 1981), p. 84.

Lowry visited the Isle of Man as a child when tourism was at its height. The period documented in the photographs included here corresponds with a decline in tourism and the timeframe of my formative experiences, from the mid-1960s to the mid-1980s, of growing up in a place which I have left, but to which I have since returned. Lowry never visited the island as an adult, but the childhood summer holiday he spent there prompted his imagination and his projection across the sea to elsewhere. Cosnahan, as an alter ego of Lowry, faces the double-bind of a kind of homelessness: in his mind, he is unable to return to his point of origin. Lowry reimagines this estrangement through warm recollections of his friend Jimmy Craige in Dollarton. Lowry's relationship with Liverpool, 'that terrible city whose main street is the ocean', and with Vancouver, was an uneasy one. The Dee estuary of his early years and the Burrard Inlet at Dollarton, in later life, provided sanctuary from the industrialised modernity of these cities; each time, amidst his psychic and physical dislocation, he attempted to make a new home where he was able to write. Consequently the ellipsis of that which slips, or has been lost, is caught up in the circulatory narrative of his displacement and runs throughout his life and writing.

In a way, though it was hard to see why, it had been like one of those forgotten but universal aftermaths to some quarrel of early marriage, arising from having drunk too much at some stupid party, escaping from which into the inevitable bar one ran into some friend of one's youth, down on his luck perhaps, but who instead of borrowing money or showing signs of renewing friendship beyond a point said, surprisingly and kindly, 'What sympathy do

you expect to get in a place like this you can't get at home, you old bastard?'
so that, although one didn't go home immediately, a little later one found that
this advice, 'Why don't you go home, you can't handle the stuff,' must really
have taken root on the spot: but in this case it was not alcohol he could not
handle, it was – and so his earlier train of thought, like Cosnahan himself in
his walk around Rome, came full circle – (pp. 172–73)

ELLIPTICAL JOURNEYS: MALCOLM LOWRY, EXILE AND RETURN

Paul Rooney, *Bellevue* (pre-production stills), 2009. The film re-presents
fragments from Lowry's *Lunar Caustic*, which is set in a psychiatric wing
of New York's Bellevue Hospital in the 1930s. Rooney's film transplants
dialogue and other texts from the book into a present-day advertising focus
group session held at an English country house.

Commissioned by Film & Video Umbrella and the Bluecoat

Lunatic city: Lowry's *Lunar Caustic* and New York

Michele Gemelos

In 1954 Malcolm Lowry wrote:

> In my own experience – *odi et amo* – that particular city – it favors brief and
> furious outbursts, but not the long haul. Moreover for all its drama and
> existential fury, or perhaps because of it, it's a city where it can be remarkably
> hard – or so it seems to me – to get on the right side of one's despair.[1]

New York was 'that particular city' where Lowry attempted (in vain) to get on
the right side of his personal and professional despair in the 1930s. Lowry and
his American wife, Jan Gabrial, had been living a turbulent expatriate literary life
in France. When Jan eventually returned to the US to visit her family, the couple
agreed she would return within months but after much alcohol-fuelled confusion
about his writing and whether to stay in France, Lowry left for England instead.
After more deliberation, it was decided that he would sail for New York to be
reunited with his wife. The numerous professional and personal challenges he faced
in Europe seemed to be pushing Lowry across the Atlantic, away from his homeland
and towards Jan. Lowry's long-standing 'love-affair' with the symbolic freedom of
America, however, contributed to that powerful westward impetus towards New
York for a brief and furious sojourn.[2]

The word 'furious' aptly characterises Lowry's somewhat extended stopover in
that city from 1934 to 1936; with the repeal of Prohibition, Lowry freely imbibed
and was much taken with the idea of life as a literary exile in a creative and
cosmopolitan sanctuary. He wrote and rewrote with fervour, but he was also
plagued by insecurities about the authenticity of his prose after a particularly
difficult encounter with an editor at Doubleday. Lowry stood accused of
plagiarising significant portions of *Ultramarine*, his first novel, and as a result he
found himself furiously revising *In Ballast to the White Sea*, the work that occupied
most of his time in New York.

Fears of this nature intensified and, although Lowry never managed to conquer his
despair about derivativeness, his engagement with New York shaped his thinking
on origins, community and selfhood, as evidenced in his novella set in the city –
Lunar Caustic. It is a catalogue of the hallucinatory, alcoholic New York wanderings
(and eventual hospitalisation) of the Cambridge-educated, self-exiled jazz musician
William ('Bill') Plantagenet. This text – and especially its genesis – also provides
insight into Lowry's views on the metropolis, modernity and belonging. It adds to

---

1   Malcolm Lowry, letter to David Markson, 1954, *Canadian Literature*, 8 (1961), pp. 42–46.
2   Gordon Bowker, *Pursued by Furies: A Life of Malcolm Lowry* (London: Harper Collins, 1993), p. 180. Bowker explains
     that the 'love-affair' began through the cinema and was intensified by Lowry's 1929 visit to his literary mentor, the
     American writer Conrad Aiken.

57

a rich history of British literary engagements with New York City that dates back to writers such as Frances Trollope and Charles Dickens, and includes twentieth-century contributions from – among many others – the travel writer Stephen Graham, the novelist Ford Madox Ford, and the poet W. H. Auden.

On 28 July 1934, his twenty-fifth birthday, Lowry left Liverpool for Southampton, where he boarded the *Aquitania* bound for New York. Significantly, this was the same ship on which his fellow English writer D. H. Lawrence had sailed westward a decade earlier, possessed by the (ultimately unfulfilled) dream of establishing a utopian community in New Mexico.[3] Lowry dreamt of escaping the 'non-creative bullyboys and homosapient schoolmasters of English Literature' – to borrow words from another Lowry protagonist, Sigbjørn Wilderness.[4] For Lowry, England generally and Liverpool specifically had come to represent a trap but also a path; in the words of his biographer Gordon Bowker, Lowry's home city was both 'the lunatic city inside which he was to feel trapped and was to suffer, and [...] the pathway to the sea and the ocean voyage, the risk-laden escape route from lunacy into uncertainty'.[5]

The uneasy relationship Lowry had with Liverpool would be reproduced, however, in New York in the 1930s; his fears and anxieties about his home town and homeland would be echoed in his adopted city. In *Writing Liverpool*, Michael Murphy and Deryn Rees-Jones locate the emergence of a distinctive Liverpool literary voice in the 1930s: as the city experienced extreme economic decline, its writers captured the city in crisis but also struggled to balance the contradictions implicit in characterising the place and its people.[6] Writing in New York, Lowry seemed to be using this kind of Liverpool voice to capture another city in similar crisis, to balance its contradictions, and to try to deal with those personal ones that he imported.

Echoing and reversing Liverpool's representation as 'America in England',[7] *Lunar Caustic*'s City hospital (as a microcosm of New York) can be seen as a little English outpost in America: reading the novella, one is made aware of Lowry's overwhelming concerns about Englishness and affiliation, articulated by Plantagenet. Lowry seems to be aware of the two cities' shared histories of wealth, supremacy and instability, and their similar, very difficult relationships with their countries, both cities often being presented as or perceived to be outsiders or alien to the nation as a whole. As gateways to empires, they can be seen as transitional or liminal places, or as frontiers.[8] They can be seen as landscapes of opportunity and

3   Malcolm Bradbury, *Dangerous Pilgrimages* (London: Penguin, 1996 [1995]), p. 388.
4   Malcolm Lowry, 'Through the Panama', in *Hear Us O Lord from Heaven Thy Dwelling Place* (London: Picador, 1993 [1961]), p. 74.
5   Bowker, *Pursued by Furies*, p. 180.
6   Michael Murphy and Deryn Rees-Jones (eds.), *Writing Liverpool: Essays and Interviews* (Liverpool: Liverpool University Press, 2007), p. 1.
7   *Writing Liverpool*, p. 8.
8   See Ralph Crane, 'A Man from Elsewhere: The Liminal Presence of Liverpool in the Fiction of J. G. Farrell', in Murphy and Rees-Jones (eds.), *Writing Liverpool*, p. 96.

fortune on the one hand, and of treachery and struggle on the other. Lowry's New York – as presented in *Lunar Caustic* and miniaturised in his presentation of the City hospital – is both curative gateway and a paralysing fortress.

Perhaps most crucially to the genesis of *Lunar Caustic*, Lowry checked into the psychiatric wing of Bellevue Hospital in May 1936. Despite the doubts raised about Lowry's sobriety and sanity during his New York years, Lowry maintained that the only reason for his ten-day stay in Bellevue was to research the conditions for a story to be titled 'Delirium on the East River'.[9] Before he was discharged (on the grounds that his alien status prevented the hospital from continuing treatment), Lowry had the seeds for a work that he continued to revise until his death in 1957.

With a volatile plot, unstable form, and problematic publication history, *Lunar Caustic* is, in the words of Douglas Day, 'happy hunting ground for a textual analyst, but frustrating work for a literary critic or biographer'.[10] The narrative, focusing on a self-destructive British journalist who is accidentally detained at a New York City hospital, was expanded and given the new title 'The Last Address' in 1936, possibly to call attention to the proximity of Bellevue to the last home of Herman Melville at 104 East 26th Street.[11] 'The Last Address' was submitted to *Story* magazine for publication but it never appeared in print there. Four years later and having moved on from New York, Lowry produced another version titled 'Swinging the Maelstrom'. This was further revised, with revamped characters and a radically different (and notably optimistic) ending. It was then published in an authorised French translation in the journal *L'Esprit* in 1956. Still dissatisfied with the English version, however, Lowry continued to splice the stories into the more ambitious form of a novella, for which he had already chosen the striking title:

> *Lunar Caustic* as a sardonic and ambiguous title for a cauterizing work on madness has, I feel, a great deal of merit. But lunar caustic is also silver nitrate and used unsuccessfully to cure syphilis. And indeed as such it might stand symbolically for any imperfect or abortive cure, for example of alcoholism.[12]

A painful treatment, silver nitrate was also used to clear the sight of infants at birth, so the title suggests Lowry's interest in revelation and re-envisioning.[13] These themes are underscored by the constant disorientation of Lowry's drunken protagonist, and the miasmic events that unfold within the hospital setting and against the cityscape.

Moreover, the textual history also reveals Lowry's obsession with 'revising' and re-envisioning his view of New York in the 1930s. By the time of his death, Lowry had planned to collect his life's writings into a Dantesque series called *The Voyage*

---

9   Bowker, *Pursued by Furies*, p. 181. See also Douglas Day, *Malcolm Lowry: A Biography* (London: Oxford University Press, 1974), pp. 192–212.
10 Day, *Malcolm Lowry: A Biography*, p. 197.
11 Bellevue is located between East 27th and 30th Streets at 1st Avenue in Manhattan.
12 Malcolm Lowry, letter to Harold Matson (4), undated, Malcolm Lowry Collection, University of British Columbia Library.
13 Keith Harrison, 'Lowry's Allusions to Melville in "Lunar Caustic"', *Canadian Literature*, 94 (1982), pp. 182, 184.

that Never Ends, of which *Lunar Caustic* would have been the 'Purgatorio' component. Although this task was not fully undertaken by his literary executors (nor by Michael Hofmann in his recent edited collection of Lowry's writing[14]), *Lunar Caustic* was resurrected in 1963 by his widow, Margerie Bonner Lowry, whom Lowry married after the disintegration of his relationship with Jan Gabrial. With the help of the Canadian poet Earle Birney, Margerie Lowry completed the task of collating the various starts and drafts, and published a version in the *Paris Review* that has become the only 'authorised' and complete text available.[15]

The novella opens as Plantagenet is ending a disorientated, drink-fuelled sojourn in New York's dockside. The narration is punctuated by Bill's nightmares. In one, his estranged American wife, Ruth, appears and initially offers him pity, 'only to be instantly transformed into Richard III, who sprang forward to smother him'. The moment can be read as a self-attack – a Plantagenet killing a Plantagenet – and certainly Plantagenet seems out to do himself harm.[16] He soon wakes to finds himself in the City hospital, which he initially mistakes for a church. While under the observation of the supervising psychiatrist-cum-ringmaster – the Melvillean Dr Claggart – Plantagenet tries to recover from the departure of his wife by befriending other patients who become his surrogate family in his new home town. He finds temporary sobriety and, feeling somewhat rejuvenated, he attempts to reform conditions within the institution.

The evolution of the plot, characterisations and dialogue illustrate Lowry's aim of exposing both the collective and the individual anxieties of the age by presenting insanity and injustice from within the structure of the City hospital, a type of ark complete with a starling range of human 'types'. Some commentators on *Lunar Caustic* have noted its overt social criticism, which is articulated through Plantagenet's pleas for greater compassion from both the hospital's staff and his fellow patients.[17] His demands are fragmented and surrealistic, confusing both the doctors and his lunatic comrades. The failure of most of his 'community' (particularly Dr Claggart) to comprehend Plantagenet allows us to see the novella as an abortive or imperfect treatment for Lowry's problems with form and expression and intensifies the sense of estrangement that prevails throughout the text.

The narrative progression of *Lunar Caustic* serves as a constant reminder that Plantagenet's identity is powerfully linked to the spaces he occupies and his relation to others. Searching for Ruth, Plantagenet arrives in New York having lost a

---

14   *The Voyage that Never Ends: Malcolm Lowry in his Own Words: Fictions, Poems, Fragments, Letters*, ed. Michael Hofmann (New York: New York Review of Books, 2007).

15   Malcolm Lowry, *Lunar Caustic*, ed. Earle Burney and Margerie Lowry, *Paris Review*, 29 (Winter/Spring 1963), pp. 15-73; the novella was published by Jonathan Cape in 1967. Quotations here are from the edition published with *Hear Us O Lord from Heaven Thy Dwelling Place* (London: Picador, 1993).

16   *Lunar Caustic*, p. 299. The name Plantagenet belongs to the dynastic succession of twelfth- to fourteenth-century kings who ruled over England and a significant portion of France. The line began with Henry II and ended with Richard III.

17   For example, see Mark Thomas, 'Rereading Lowry's "Lunar Caustic"', *Canadian Literature*, 112 (1987), pp. 195-97.

partner as well as his place in the world. His livelihood is music performance, but he has also lost this outlet as his group has disbanded. Plantagenet's desperate, dipsomaniacal cry outside the hospital – 'I am sent to save my father, to find my son, to heal the eternal horror of three, to resolve the immedicable horror of opposites' (p. 296) – throws him into a flawed fraternity with the patients on the ward, but this fraternity – and the terms of his internment – also restricts his freedom. He soon begins to act in accordance with the strange and complex regal significance of his 'English' surname: like an exiled foreign king, Plantagenet soon reigns over the ward, enchanting some of the inmates (or 'subjects') with tales of his exotic travels, his rebellious attitude and his piano playing.

Plantagenet also records his fellow patients' ritual of gazing out from their prison-house onto the city:

> Every so often, when a ship passed, there would be a curious mass movement towards the barred windows, a surging whose source was in the breasts of the mad seamen and firemen there, but to which all were tributary: even those whose heads had been bowed for days rose at this stirring, their bodies shaking as though roused suddenly from nightmare or from the dead, while their lips would burst with a sound, partly a cheer and partly a wailing shriek, like some cry of the imprisoned spirit of New York itself, that spirit haunting the abyss between Europe and America and brooding like futurity over the Western Ocean. (pp. 297-98)

In this passage, the patients give voice to the 'imprisoned spirit of New York itself', suggesting a divorce between the physical reality of the city and the essence, or soul, of the city which they embody for Plantagenet: seething, furious, but ultimately trapped. Their attempts to communicate with the ships – signifying paths to freedom – are futile. And yet the passage suggests the future and freedom as dark, cacophonous and riotous. At these moments Plantagenet senses 'the shadow of a city of dreadful night without splendour that fell on his soul; and how darkly it felt whenever a ship passed!' (pp. 304, 306).

In his study of British travel writing, Paul Fussell cites Sigmund Freud's 1937 assertion that 'a great part of the pleasure of travel lies in the fulfillment of [...] early wishes to escape the family and especially the father'.[18] Although this may have been part of Lowry's motivation to sail (yet again) away from home, his exploration of fraternal and familial bonds in *Lunar Caustic* suggests an equally powerful desire to re-create the family on his own terms – and his difficulties in achieving this in New York. Lowry creates a surrogate (but notably motherless) family for Plantagenet: Mr Kalowsky, an older Jewish man, becomes a type of (grand)fatherly figure and Garry, a young boy 'imprisoned' for manslaughter, becomes the son. In various conversations, Lowry creates situations in which Plantagenet and his Englishness (or Plantagenet as representative of Englishness) are presented as paternalistic and yet palliative:

---

18   Paul Fussell, *Abroad: British Literary Travelling Between the Wars* (New York: Oxford University Press, 1982), p. 15.

Mr Kalowsky, sensing and giving utterance to Plantagenet's silent concern for Garry's welfare, exclaims, 'You shouldn't be here, Garry [...] You'll only get worser here – whatever do they want to put you here for? [...] – when you should be reading the works of Dickens?' with a polite nod to Bill, as if he implied, 'the great Englishman.' (p. 311)

Garry reveals that he too is enchanted by his own dream of a Romantic, pastoral 'Elengland'. Garry's mispronunciation of Plantagenet's homeland signifies his misunderstanding about the realities of the England from which Bill has fled:

'And I know Elengland too,' he addressed Bill. 'After you've seen the doctor, I'll tell you, you'll take us to Elengland. Mr Kalowsky and I and maybe my brother; I can see it all plainly. There are some farms there. I know I might see artists on the hillside or cows and sheep grazing in green pastures. I can see them there, the artists, painting pictures of flowers and the different birds and the mountains and the lakes and trees. Or,' he dropped his voice, 'you might go to one part where an artist is painting pictures of ruins.'
(pp. 311-12)

In Garry's ironically innocent eyes, the dipsomaniacal Plantagenet is a type of creative saviour who will lead them out through the gate of the New World, all the way back to the green and pleasant Old World. Plantagenet does not recoil from them or this revised version of his homeland, but remarks that it 'seems strange to me that I should have to come all the way from England to a madhouse to find two people I really care about' (p. 331) – and who, it should be noted, really care about who he is and where he is from. Remarkably early in his 'commitment', he reveals to Dr Claggart that he and his estranged wife Ruth suffered transatlantic enchantments and disenchantments:

Hell with her! She only brought me back as a sort of souvenir from Europe. Perhaps it was America I was in love with. You know, you people get sentimental over England from time to time with your guff about sweetest Shakespeare. Well, this was the other way round. Only it was Eddie Lang and Joe Venuti and the death of Bix [...] And I wanted to see where Melville lived. You'll never know how disappointed I was not to find any whalers in New Bedford. (pp. 302–303)

Throughout *Lunar Caustic*, exchanges about and juxtapositions of English and American culture have the effect of foregrounding Plantagenet's thwarted expectations of New York and his abiding concerns with origins, affiliation and belonging. As Plantagenet's haunting continues,

[he] looked over the huge nervous city above which the last blimp of the day was trailing an advertisement for Goodyear Tyres, while far above that in still merciless but declining sunlight one word was unrolling itself from the wake of an invisible plane: *Fury*. He was afraid. [...] 'The horrors,' he said abruptly. 'Well – do you see New York? That's where they are. They're out there waiting, the horrors of war – all of them – already – and all that delirium,

like primitives, like Christ's descent into hell. And the tactile conscience, the lonely soul falling featherless into the abyss!' (p. 51)

By revealing these horrible visions of the city to Dr Claggart, Plantagenet reveals his fear about rejoining the world outside the hospital – a lonely world devoid of the fraternity or familial bonds that he has developed, paradoxically, while being confined with madmen. His paranoia about 'alienating' freedom intensifies as he is reminded of the paralysing bonds of his past:

> And it's all there waiting for me: the ghosts on the window blind, the scarlet snowshoe, the whispering of lost opportunities, and all the fury, the anguish, the remorse, the voices, voices, voices, voices; the doll that turns to Ruth, the brownstone – brimstone – fronts transformed into judges, the interminable helpful but – alas – non-existent conversations, clinching one's case and pointing a solution, a way out into the morning light and freedom, offering you an outpost between yourself and death [...] (p. 334)

By the end of *Lunar Caustic*, the city has amplified, rather than mollified, Plantagenet's concerns about his past and his future. As he listens to the elevated railway, '[the] roar of the train seemed to be trying to communicate with him. First it said "womb", then "tomb". Then it said both in succession, very rapidly, over and over again' (p. 345). It is as if the city suggests to Plantagenet that it may potentially provide a surrogate home, but that 'home' could easily become one's final resting place.

As Malcolm Bradbury has noted, the womb was a troubling metaphor for many writers in the 1930s. Bradbury suggests that the search for consolation from spiritual, sexual and political unease led many writers to explore the image of the double womb: 'the womb toward which we regress, avoiding rebirth' and 'the world as womb, permitting the rebirth of the individual being and consciousness'.[19] In this sense, the metropolis of New York – the mother city – into which Plantagenet is forced after his expulsion from the hospital becomes that regressive womb. It contrasts with the womb of the City hospital, where Plantagenet was, if only temporarily, reborn as an individual and where he tried to reconnect with his consciousness. Perhaps fittingly, it is his alien status – his Englishness – that forces his expulsion. The novella ends with a sense of futility and paralysis overwhelming all of Plantagenet's original 'reformist' impulses. Returning to the dockside saloons where he began his New York sojourn, Plantagenet retreats, 'drink in hand, to the very obscurest corner of the bar, where, curled up like an embryo, he could not be seen at all' (p. 346).

Looking back at Lowry's revisions of *Lunar Caustic*, 'The Last Address' also concludes with overwhelming despair and paralysis. In contrast, the ending of 'Swinging the Maelstrom' shows that Lowry was working towards a hopeful

---

19   Bradbury, *Dangerous Pilgrimages*, pp. 380–81.

resolution of his protagonist's conflict – in fact, the version he submitted to *L'Esprit* for translation has much more in common with 'Swinging the Maelstrom' than with that version's predecessors, further suggesting that the impression of New York City that Lowry wished to put into print might have been brief and furious but was not one of long-lasting futility.

Among the many questions about the fragments of *Lunar Caustic* which remain unanswered is why Margerie Lowry and Earle Birney retained the original despair-filled ending. In a 1952 letter to Albert Erskine, Lowry admitted that he saw his incomplete novella as 'too gruesome for anyone's consumption. I can even now believe that my unconscious made it too gruesome for anyone whatever but I cannot believe that there is no merit in it.'[20] The loss of a hopeful ending enhances the gruesome quality of the impressions, but the text of *Lunar Caustic* that is readily available to readers today occludes Lowry's full, complex and fluctuating vision of New York. The different versions of *Lunar Caustic* merit more attention: the text we read today is the result of Lowry's struggle with language, form and identity, and his literary executors' struggle with the puzzles of authorial intention. The permutations of the stories leading to *Lunar Caustic* illustrate important metamorphoses in Lowry's view of New York City as it became a *locus desperatus* for a nascent novella.

20   Malcolm Lowry, letter to Albert Erskine, March 1952, in *Selected Letters of Malcolm Lowry*, ed. Harvey Breit and Margerie Bonner Lowry (London: Jonathan Cape, 1967), p. 290.

Julian Cooper, *Bella Vista Hotel*, 1982, oil on canvas, 137 x 183 cm

Arts Council Collection, Southbank Centre, London

Julian Cooper, *On the Porch*, 1983, oil on canvas, 122 x 184 cm

Collection of Sandra Blythe

Julian Cooper, *Yvonne – the Consul's wife*, 1984, oil on canvas, 122 x 163 cm
Collection of the Artist

Murals by Chambas in the Palace of Fine Arts underground station, Mexico City
Photographs by Alberto Rebollo

'It is not Mexico of course, but in the heart...': Lowry seen from Quauhnáhuac

Alberto Rebollo

> Ghosts. Ghosts, as at the Casino, certainly lived here.
>
> Malcolm Lowry, *Under the Volcano*

I. *Under the Volcano*

When I first read *Under the Volcano* there came a moment in which a very strange sensation came to me, a kind of 'literary *déjà vu*': I felt as if I somehow had already known the story, as if I somehow had been there in it. Then I made the melancholy of the story my own – especially when Yvonne and Hugh go riding horses across the forest and they stop to drink a freezing bottle of Carta Blanca.[1] I felt as if I were one of Lowry's characters (Hugh maybe) lost in some Mexican countryside spot, starting to drink, with all day ahead of me, feeling as free as possible and with that special sense of calm, slowness and thoughtfulness that one can feel in the countryside, away from the traffic and crowded Mexico City, full of policemen trying to stop you drinking outdoors, a situation my generation could only avoid by going out of the enormous city, to places like Cuernavaca (Lowry's Quauhnáhuac). It must be because there are so many elements in *Under the Volcano* that appeal to a Mexican reader like me – being a strong drinker myself, in love with the sea, a kind of idealist, an activist for the poor, with a special background in English literature and who dreams with a perfect love – that I have never felt so close to a work of fiction. Maybe also because I have always felt like a stranger in my own land, for example when I see certain kinds of behaviour I can't understand and which shock me every day. For it deals with the relationship between an outsider, a *mezcal* drinker, and a mysterious and macabre Mexican world. But above all, because I am fascinated with the traditions of my people, especially with those of the Day of the Dead. It is really a curiosity that my countrymen revere all kinds of saints, as for example the so-called Saint Death,[2] which is now widely celebrated in Mexican communities in the United States. Perhaps it was the mixture of these two elements, my personal background and my fascination with Mexican traditions, that made me feel so hooked on the book. I have always had the impression that in Mexico there is a sense of tragedy that is deeply rooted in the land itself. Reading any newspaper you will find a dozen tragedies a day, and that seems to have been so since ancient times. Death has always been present in Mexico as an element of cult; it is related

---

[1]   Carta Blanca is a Mexican beer brewed by the Cuauhtémoc-Moctezuma brewery.

[2]   Saint Death or Holy Death is a figure with a cult following in Mexico today. The figure, which seems to have pre-Hispanic origins, is celebrated by all kinds of people, but above all by gangsters and narcotics dealers. I would see it as the perfect icon of the Mexican celebration of tragedy.

to the religiousness of the people. From a Mexican perspective, Lowry's greatest achievement in my opinion was that he was able, even more than any Mexican, to depict the importance of the cult of the ancestors and the idea of death itself. He also provided the answer: human solidarity against death, human solidarity against isolation and the devastation of the world, understanding among the peoples of the world; and he did that in the tenderest possible way, so that no one in Mexico has ever felt offended by his depiction of Mexico and the Mexicans. He is 'constructing a place, not describing one; he is making a Mexico for the mind',[3] as William Gass says. Lowry uses Mexico as the perfect setting for his novel, a kind of pretext to present a story, a fable, an allegory that is in the end a comedy and a tragedy that could apply to any human being living in our present-day consumer societies, an era of clinical depression, drugs, war, devastation, and suicide.

Lowry was able to depict quite precisely the character of my countrymen and the desolation of a foreigner who is confronted with the reality of Mexico. Lowry is able to convey the sadness intrinsic to Mexico, the strong influence of the past that one can feel here and that Lowry approaches so well, much better than most Mexicans have done. His descriptions of the rural atmosphere in a desolate and dusty volcanic place are as frightening as Juan Rulfo's views in *Pedro Paramo*, or in *The Burning Plain and Other Stories*, where we can read his tale: 'Tell them not to kill me'.[4] Lowry was also able to see the spirits of the dead who do live in Mexico and somehow bring them into his book; it is full of them, they inhabit it: 'Ghosts. Ghosts, as at the Casino, certainly lived here',[5] thinks M. Laruelle while walking outside the Cortez[6] Palace. Ramón Sender says that in Mexico 'mythology is still alive in the streets, not merely in folkloric terms but in the folds of the air seen only by poets, children, and an occasional madman'.[7] That is especially true in the work of particularly sensitive writers, such as Lowry. Carlos Fuentes says:

> Art in Mexico [...] has always been allied to mythology. [...] [The] physical nature of Mexico – a cruel, devouring, sunbaked landscape – is filled with portents of magical distraction. Every force of nature seems to have a mythical equivalent in Mexico. No other nation is quite so totemic [...] Whether creating a stone pedestal for the worship of the earth goddess Coatlique, a gilded temple honoring [the Virgin of] Guadalupe, a novel defending the underdog or a mural recalling the heroic past, the

3   William Gass, cited in Chris Ackerley, *A Companion to Under the Volcano* (Vancouver: University of British Columbia Press, 1984), p. 3.
4   Rulfo is one of the most celebrated authors of Mexico and Latin America. Although he published only two books, he was very influential on García Márquez as well as on many other writers.
5   Malcolm Lowry, *Under the Volcano* (New York: Perennial Classics, 2000), p. 15.
6   The correct spelling is 'Cortés'. Lowry misspells many of his references in Spanish and also mistranslates many: for example, *farolito* does not mean (as he thought) 'little light-house', but 'little street lamp'; 'little light-house' would be *farito*.
7   Ramón Sender, cited in Ronald Walker, *Infernal Paradise: Mexico and the Modern English Novel* (Berkeley: University of California Press, 1978), p. 13.

MALCOLM LOWRY: FROM THE MERSEY TO THE WORLD

Mexican artist has seldom been able to act outside the demands of the all-encompassing myth.[8]

Many foreign scholars tend to think that Lowry merely used Mexico as the setting of his novel, and concentrate their studies on the literary, philosophical, cinematic, political, and even cabbalistic implications of the book; but, save Walker, they do not dig deeper into the significance of the Mexican people, traditions, landscapes and cultures for the novel, and their importance for our understanding of it. García Ponce, the Mexican writer, once said that only a person who spoke perfect English, and the Spanish of Mexico, and who knew Mexico and England, would be able to understand *Under the Volcano* in a complete sense, given that there are a great number of mistranslations, puns and allusions to Mexican history,[9] and he was not far wrong. *Under the Volcano* is not only a 'bilingual' book but a 'bicultural' book, and we discover much more through a bicultural reading of it.

Such a reading could start with the fact that the Day of the Dead is absolutely central to the final sense of the tragedy: it is the day when the dead return, and almost the whole book is about a couple who are dead from the very beginning of the book, but who return and tell their story. Therefore Yvonne and Geoffrey are still here, alive, loving each other like the eternal lovers Popocatépetl and Ixtaccíhuatl, always present in the *Volcano*'s landscape: 'the perfect marriage'. We believe that they return to Cuernavaca to drink with us – *mezcal*, of course – on the Day of the Dead. They are also immortal in the sense in which artists are immortal: Lowry and his characters (who at the same time are real people) are immortal now because of his work. This double immortality is one of the most striking things in Lowry's myth.

What astonished us as Mexican fans of Lowry is the extraordinary way that he transformed and mythologised the actual geography of Cuernavaca and its surroundings, its landscapes, its historic buildings and even its places of recreation. This transformation is so wonderful that every time we are in those places – Cortés Palace, the Borda Gardens, the Cathedral, Cine Morelos, the ravines – we see them as 'sacred' because (as Douglas Day notes[10]) *Under the Volcano* is a religious novel, and they also remind us of the bittersweet nature of life and of the fact that we have no option but to leave a testimony to the world of our brief existence.

II The Mexican characters and Mexico

It is true that in the *Volcano*, there are some descriptions or passages which seem to suggest a somewhat racist view of Mexican characters, such as the case of the *cartero*

---

8   Walker, *Infernal Paradise*, pp. 12-13.
9   For example the Tlaxcalan traitors who helped the Spanish against the Aztecs during the conquest of these territories.
10   In fact Day describes *Under the Volcano* as 'the greatest religious novel of [the twentieth] century'; Douglas Day, *Malcolm Lowry: A Biography* (Oxford: Oxford University Press, 1973), p. 350.

– postman – at the end of chapter six; yet Lowry also noted in a letter that he was keen to write a prologue to the *Volcano* in which he could clear up some possible misunderstandings relating to his depiction of Mexicans in the *Volcano*. In the case of the postman there is a clear external point of view of him as the man who 'walks on all fours', which is mainly how Yvonne and Hugh see him, but on the other hand he seems very friendly and to have something important to give: 'Hugh too was waiting expectantly, not so much any word from the Globe, which would come if at all by cable, but half in hope, plausible, of another minuscule Oaxaqueñan envelope, covered with bright stamps of archers shooting at the sun, from Juan Cerillo' (p. 200). That is, he connects his friend Juan Cerillo, a heroic Oaxaqueñan, with this 'grotesque little creature' (p. 199), which means that Hugh in the end respects the man. Moreover, as we know, Juan Cerillo is related in Lowry's world to Juan Fernando Márquez, the hero and dedicatee of Lowry's next novel *Dark as the Grave wherein My Friend is Laid*. Moreover, at the end of the book Hugh has become 'really indistinguishable from a Mexican now' (p. 285). The Consul himself mentions several times that he would like to go to live with the Indians like William Blackstone, which in a way refuses the European conqueror's position towards the Indians and the evil world the 'conquerors' have created: 'Ah, what a world it was, that trampled down the truth and drunkards alike!' (p. 88).

Many of the Mexicans in the novel seem to be just part of the landscape, flitting through the Consul's mind like ghosts, creating an atmosphere of desolation, centred on the Consul, who is enclosed in his own exile and seems to want to be alone. However, some Mexicans play a more active role in the story. Dr Vigil is the Consul's best friend, whom he drinks with at the Red Cross party. He is the one who takes him to the church to pray to 'the Virgin for those who have nobody with' for his wife to come back. The doctor tries to take him out of hell (Quauhnáhuac) and to Guanajuato, so that he can dry out, but the Consul refuses. Dr Vigil is like the Consul's father in the sense that he helps and guides his steps during his last journey.

Lowry's vision of the native people is one of contrasts. Sometimes they are exalted: 'Their voices, the gestures of their refined grimy hands, were unbelievably courtly, delicate. Their carriage suggested the majesty of Aztec princes, their faces obscure sculpturings on Yucatecan ruins' (p. 12). They are even credited with having developed a great culture: 'the Conquest took place in a civilisation which was as good if not better than that of the conquerors, a deep-rooted structure' (p. 310); '"The Mayas," he read aloud, "were far advanced in observational astronomy. But they did not suspect a Copernican system"' (p. 84). But at other times they are seen as stupid. In the morning, for example, while travelling to Parián on the bus, the Consul thinks, 'No one could be more courageous than a Mexican. But this was not clearly a situation demanding courage' (p. 258); the apparent exaltation of the courage of the Mexican is transformed into criticism when the Consul thinks that this moment demands, more than courage, temper and intelligence. When the Consul feels threatened in the Farolito, he thinks, 'The only trouble was one was very much afraid these particular Indians might turn out to be people with ideas too' (p. 370). The Consul refers here to the *sinarquistas*, a far-right mafia who control the Farolito and who also robbed and probably killed the Indian. They are the devil: they are Mexicans, but they are the worst of this society.

Nevertheless, ultimately the most important thing seems to be love for this land, '[originally] settled by a scattering of those fierce forbears of Cervantes who had succeeded in making Mexico great even in her betrayal, the traitorous Tlaxcalans' (p. 295). This also seems to be a response to other writers, such as D. H. Lawrence and his *Plumed Serpent*: in the *Volcano* Mexico is an important developed culture and this crazy drunkard is able to see it, in contrast with Lawrence's European conqueror who saw here only savage people. The character who synthesises this clearly is William Blackstone, who rejected 'civilisation' to live 'among the Indians'.

In the morning, at Señora Gregorio's place, the Consul thinks, in relation to the Mexicans, 'Earlier it had been the insects; now these were closing in upon him again, these animals, these people without ideas' (pp. 237–38). Moreover, he becomes angry when Señora Gregorio mispronounces English: 'Not sank you, Señora Gregorio, thank you' (p. 239). But Señora Gregorio is much more than a simple woman in the cantina, she is almost like his mother:

> He held out his hand, then dropped it – Good God, what had come over him? For an instant he'd thought he was looking at his own mother. Now he found himself struggling with his tears, that he wanted to embrace Señora Gregorio, to cry like a child, to hide his face on her bosom. 'Adiós,' he said, and seeing a tequila on the counter just the same, he drank it rapidly. (pp. 238-39)

In fact, their relationship is based on 'shared misery' (p. 236): both bear a great sadness for the past.

Maria, the prostitute in the Farolito, is described as a perfect woman for temptation: the Consul 'saw only the shapely legs of the girl [... he] saw she was young and pretty' (pp. 360, 361). The contrast is to the Consul's impotence with his wife, who is also beautiful. Acting as the *conquistador*, he has sex with the 'Indian', but here, as it were, as part of a deliberate betrayal of his wife: Maria appears on the surface to be a character of little importance, but she is Yvonne's counterpart.

Another important Mexican woman in the novel is the old lady of Tarasco, the lady of the dominoes. The Consul accuses Yvonne of being unable to see 'the beauty of an old woman from Tarasco who plays dominoes at seven o'clock in the morning'. In fact Yvonne sees her as an 'evil omen' (p. 52). This old lady plays a magic role in the novel: she foresees the Consul's future in the dominoes and tries to help him. At the end the Consul realises that she has been helping all the time. She asks him to go away but he refuses and is ready to die. He wants to die as a hero, trying to free the Indian's horse; he is indeed killed by the mafia outside the Farolito, but

73

'IT IS NOT MEXICO OF COURSE, BUT IN THE HEART...': LOWRY SEEN FROM QUAUHNAHUAC

La vida intra-dimensional de Lowry

Lowry´s intra-dimensional life

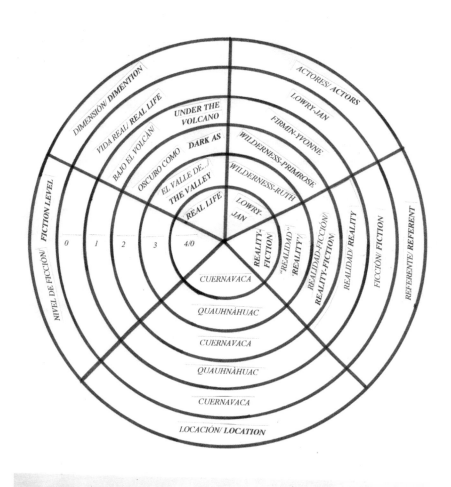

'someone had called him "compañero" too, which was better, much better. It made him happy' (p. 387). He dies as a comrade in the front line, being blessed by Hugh, perhaps, or by the old lady. The book ends with the words, 'Somebody threw a dead dog after him down the ravine'. In the Aztec and other traditions the dog is the animal that accompanies the dead on their way to Mictlán, the obscure region. The dog must go with the Consul to help him, but also the dog is an anagram of the word 'god'. Geoffrey, then, goes with God to his domain, helped by the Aztec dog.

Thus, the Mexican characters, who may appear to play minor roles in the novel, are ultimately the Consul's father, mother, best friend, lover and 'godmother' – his whole family, though Yvonne seems to hate them all, unable to see any sign of goodness in any of them. But Mexico stands as a metaphor for the world. In a way it is irrelevant to discuss the precise role of the country as the setting of the novel: the stage of the tragedy is finally the world, which shows the worst of human nature:

' [...] first, Spaniard exploits Indian, then, when he had children, he exploited the halfbreed, then the pureblooded Mexican Spaniard, the *criollo*, then the *mestizo* exploits everybody, foreigners, Indians, and all. Then the Germans and Americans exploited him: now the final chapter, the exploitation of everybody by everybody else – ' (p. 310)

The Consul is angry with the political situation of the world. This is why he identifies himself with the poor, the Indian, especially with the 'old lame Indian' who appears at the end of chapter 9, carrying on his back 'another poor Indian, yet older and more decrepit than himself' (p. 290). In the end the Consul wants to be a Mexican subject, to live with the Indians.

III. *Dark as the Grave*

Some years after my reading of *Under the Volcano*, I came to read *Dark as the Grave wherein My Friend is Laid*, and, as I read it, I was amazed to discover that Lowry had created a kind of play of Chinese boxes: there was a story inside another story, which was inside another story, which was inside another one, and so on *ad infinitum*. Under the spell of the *Volcano*, he was able both to transform a character of his own fiction into a real person (Janet from *Ultramarine* into Jan, his wife), and also to transfigure himself into a character of his own fiction: the Consul. (He may even have been murdered, like his *alter ego* in *Under the Volcano*...) Lowry's personal life is alive in his novels and his novels influenced his actions in real life – so it is perfectly natural and logical that people often find it difficult to separate fact from fiction in Lowry's case. I have created a schema in which I show this game of Chinese boxes, the Lowryan literary play. In Lowryan terms it would be something like an 'intra-dimensional life'. Here we can see more clearly Lowry's play of mirrors, a labyrinth in which we go directly towards chaos: a spiral into Hell.

IV Ripe, East Sussex

On 27 June 2007, I travelled to Ripe, East Sussex to attend a symposium on Lowry at Sussex University and to visit Lowry's grave to commemorate the fiftieth anniversary of his death. When I got to the village, I was lost, so I asked for directions to the churchyard. Weeds grew over the entrance, and therefore it was darker than the rest of the village. It was a fresh and calm afternoon, but as I was about to cross the threshold, I had the feeling of being an actor in a film or in a dream. I was assaulted by a macabre fear which, nevertheless, invited me to proceed. A pale and solemn church seemed to welcome me as old Dracula did Jonathan to his castle. There were some scholars who showed me the place and I stood solemnly by the grave for a few seconds. Then I crouched down by the grave and thanked Lowry for his legacy, but didn't know what else to do. Then I remembered Lowry saying a prayer for his dead friend, Juan Fernando Márquez, and so I said a prayer for him too. Then I opened an Ultramarine *mezcal* bottle and tipped it to Lowry, to Lowry's grave, and drank some myself. I did the same with an Indio beer and with an Anís del mono bottle. Then I lit an Alas cigarette (for him) and smoked one myself. The wind was now blowing strongly and a soft rain started to fall from the sky. Suddenly thunder began to break the tranquillity of the ceremony, and the cigarette on the grave began to burn down quickly. Some scholars who weren't worried about the rain and were still standing by the grave were surprised by the fact that it seemed that Lowry was smoking the cigarette, but I said, 'Of course, we're smoking it.' After that I said a *see you soon* to Lowry and went to the White Cottage where I took some pictures, then on to the Lamb pub, where I ended *perfectamente borracho* talking with other guests. But a scholar questioned me about my talking to Lowry at the grave; he said it was useless to speak to a dead person. He didn't know that for us Mexicans there is no borderline between the world of the living and the world of the dead; that's why we quite often go to churchyards and take presents to the dead and talk to them about the news, laugh and even eat with them. Even if we aren't Catholic this is a cult we all share as a tradition, as a natural conception of our dead. As García Márquez states in *One Hundred Years of Solitude*, written in Mexico shortly after he had read *Under the Volcano*, he who has no dead in the earth belongs nowhere. In the Lowryan language the thunder meant he was there with us, saying thanks for the *mezcal* and the Alas cigarette. To deny this would be a nonsense.

Alberto Rebollo anointing Lowry's grave at Ripe in Sussex with *mezcal*, 2007

Image courtesy of Alberto Rebollo

'IT IS NOT MEXICO OF COURSE, BUT IN THE HEART...': LOWRY SEEN FROM QUAUHNAHUAC

Cisco Jiménez, *Two Atoms Connected*, 2007,
carved wood, glass, plastic, 90 x 56 x 60 cm
Collection of the Artist

RIGHT:
Cisco Jiménez, *Peddler*, 1998,
mixed media installation: metal structure, carved wood heads,
acrylic on wood and antique frame paintings, 170 x 150 x 100 cm
Collection of the Artist

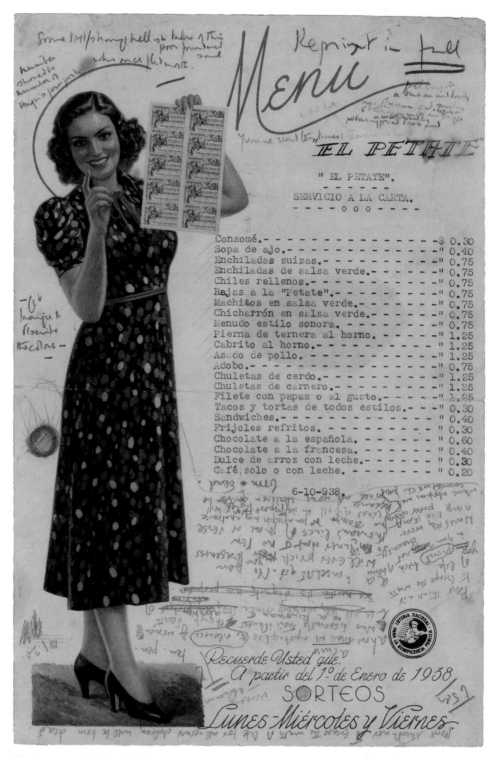

Cantina menu, with handwritten annotations by Lowry

'Lowrytrek': towards a psychogeography of Malcolm Lowry's Wirral

Mark Goodall

> Like a man stomping with heavy steps towards a murder, towards Caldy,
> towards Hoylake, along the sandy edge of the links, then at the last minute
> veering away, and down the Mersey to Paradise Street.[1]

One of the finest, and most succinct, definitions of psychogeography was
printed in the first edition of the journal *Internationale Situationniste* (June 1958):
'Psychogeography: the study of the specific effects of the geographical environment,
consciously organised or not, on the emotions of individuals'.[2] The document
was unsigned but numerous experiments utilising this method, developed out
of Surrealism and the practices of Baudelaire's *flâneur*, appeared thereafter,
contributing to an intriguing if haphazard bolus. When seeking out a new way of
approaching the works of the British writer Malcolm Lowry, the psychogeographic
mode seems to me to be extremely useful. This is particularly true when attempting
to associate in some way Lowry's stories, letters and poems with the geographical
locations that they were born out of (in this instance one of the most important
locations, Lowry's birthplace on the Wirral peninsula). This landscape clearly had a
profound effect on the young Lowry and impregnated not just his early writings but
also his whole imaginary journey along 'The Voyage That Never Ends'.

Why do a psychogeography of Malcolm Lowry? Perhaps in order to answer Brian
O'Kill's question: 'why does nobody write like this anymore?[3] O'Kill identifies a
peculiar problem with reading Lowry 'eighty years on', born out of the observation
that Lowry's influences, style and perceptions look to the past (Melville, Poe,
Gogol) yet are at the same time 'modern' even 'beyond modernism [...] a precursor
of today's postmodernism'. Lowry's writings are complex, mysterious, archaic and
experimental. Lowry's unique style cannot be read in conventional literary critical
modes, and this is perhaps why his work has faded so rapidly from the general
critical canon (in the same way that the early Surrealist and Expressionist models of
reading that Lowry revered were replaced by more 'ideological' models of criticism).
Perhaps anyway Lowry answers the question himself in one of his early letters (to
his mentor Conrad Aiken) when he orders himself: 'I must [...] identify a finer scene:

---

1   Conrad Aiken, *Ushant* (London: W. H. Allen, 1963), p. 7.
2   'Definitions', in Libero Andreotti and Xavier Costa (eds.), *Theory of the Dérive and Other Situationist Writings on the City*
     (Barcelona: Museu d'Art Contemporani de Barcelona, 1996), pp. 68-71.
3   Brian O'Kill, 'Why Does Nobody Write Like This Anymore?', in Sue Vice (ed.), *Malcolm Lowry Eighty Years On*
     (London: Macmillan, 1989), pp. 9-17.

I must in other words give an imaginary scene identity through an immediate sensation of actual experience'.[4]

That scene is psychogeographical.

This essay therefore attempts an introductory approach to Lowry's texts and to the landscape of his life from a psychogeographical perspective. A text is only part of the effect. The rest must be achieved out in the 'real' world with a pair of stout boots, one of Lowry's books and a hip flask of very strong drink.

It's no surprise that, with its emphasis on imagination, movement, mysticism and consciousness, psychogeography has recently been adopted as a means of interpreting literary texts. The psychogeographic approach can sniff out hidden aspects of a writer's work; but, importantly, it can also take the reader of Lowry's texts away from the page and into the 'real' environment. The trick is to import some aspects of the text (fragments, poetry, illustrations, lists, images) with you into the landscape. Then, augmented by the physical world and any stimulus that the drifter wishes to partake of, the world opens up and the difference between dreams and reality becomes less clear. Lowry, of course, did a superb job of transporting the reader into different and unusual worlds (even if these were of the self) and really can't be bettered. But a trip through Lowry's physical world acts as an extra dimension to his words and expressions.

Psychogeography provides the opportunity for experimenting with a particular geographical location. Guy Debord wrote that '[p]sychogeography, retaining a rather pleasing vagueness, can thus be applied to the findings arrived at by this type of investigation, to their influence on human feelings, and even more generally to any situation or conduct that seems to reflect the same spirit of discovery'.[5] The variety of possible combinations of ambience in a curious place like the Wirral peninsula 'gives rise to feelings as differentiated and complex as any form of spectacle can evoke'. The Wirral can be a place as weird and disturbing as any textual fantasy.

It is true that most 'psychogeographical' experiments have taken place within the urban environment: capital cities such as Paris or London for example. But there is no reason why a place such as Merseyside cannot be effective for psychogeographical exploration. George Melly (a native of Liverpool) once noted London's failure to establish itself as a centre for Surrealism, ascribing this to the city's 'masculinity' and 'oafishness'.[6] Melly's argument – that 'Surrealism [...] has lodged principally in provincial minds' – supports the idea that places such as Liverpool are ripe for psychogeographical experimentation. Furthermore, it is possible that a *rural* location can yield interesting and significant psychogeographical occurrences, as a drift

4   *Selected Letters of Malcom Lowry*, ed. Harvey Breit and Margerie Bonner Lowry (Harmondsworth: Penguin, 1985), p. 8.

5   Guy Debord, 'Introduction to a Critique of Urban Geography', in Andreotti and Costa (eds.), *Theory of the Dérive*, pp. 18–21.

6   George Melly and Michael Wood, *Paris and the Surrealists* (London: Thames and Hudson, 1991), p. 63.

across, to and around the Wirral peninsula will prove.[7] Although Lowry portrayed his childhood on the Wirral as one of 'perpetual gloom' (to quote his brother Russell), the proximity of nature and the sea to this home had a marked effect on his work. To some extent, Lowry's sensitive nature thrived in such a peaceful place, an escape from the urban environment in which he felt ill at ease.

The Consul on the Left Bank

Of all the writers admired by the theorists of psychogeography – the Situationist International (SI), and their precursors the Lettrist International (LI), both radical groups of mid-twentieth-century thinkers, artists, poets, madmen and drunks – Malcolm Lowry particularly stands out. In a letter to Patrick Straram sent on the Day of the Dead in 1960, Guy Debord (chief theorist of the SI) wrote: 'I had the occasion, and the time, to reread it [*Under the Volcano*] entirely, toward the beginning of September, on a train between Munich and Gênes. I had found it more fine, and more intelligent, than in 1953 despite loving it a lot then.'[8] Many of the Situationists lived their lives in imitation of Lowry's anti-hero, the Consul (and therefore perhaps of Lowry himself). One of the few English members of the collective, Ralph Rumney, a tall and well-read painter, was even nicknamed 'the Consul' by French members of the group. The Consul's words from *Under the Volcano* – 'Nothing in the world was more terrible than an empty bottle! Unless it was an empty glass' – articulate a philosophy favoured for the SI's numerous drunken *dérives* (the practice of drifting through geographical spaces in an experimental manner) about the less salubrious districts of Paris. An entire chapter of Debord's autobiography was devoted to the Lowry/Consul-esque notion that 'there is nothing like beer to straighten you out'.

Both the LI and the SI took from Lowry his superb technique in capturing the human spirit in crisis and the failure of 'modern man' to come to terms with the awfulness of contemporary existence. However, like Lowry, and the characters in his works, they seek out and find small fragments of salvation in nature, poetry, love, alcohol. Lowry's characters commonly enjoy or endure 'a technique of transient passage through varied ambiences'. For the LI and the SI this amounted to a 'mode of experimental behaviour linked to the conditions of urban society'; Lowry's characters escape to the wilderness away from the city (think of 'Eridanus' in 'Forest Path to the Spring') but this is not entirely contradictory. Debord later retired to an austere part of the Auvergne, his final parting shot to the spectacle he had always despised.

The alcoholic figure moves in and out of reality, perceiving the human condition for 'what it is' and recounting the responses to this of a 'doomed man'. In Paris, like

---

7   A Lowry *dérive* in Liverpool and on the Wirral is one of the events planned as part of the Lowry centenary festival which this book accompanies.

8   Quoted in Andy Merrifield, *Guy Debord* (London: Reaktion Books, 2005), p. 155.

Debord, Lowry showed a 'marked preference for those dim taverns off the beaten track, little frequented unless by a handful of workmen in dungarees'.[9] The trap that all humans find themselves within is evident in *Under the Volcano* as it is in the later writings and films of Debord. Both Debord and Lowry felt estranged from their 'designated' roles: Debord regularly called himself a filmmaker while Lowry insisted on being described as a poet. For both, alcoholism was an antidote: 'Gin and orange juice best cure for alcoholism real cause of which is ugliness and complete baffling sterility of existence as sold to you', Lowry once wrote, a philosophy with which the French radicals and their critiques of post-war capitalism would surely concur.[10]

It was not Debord, however, but the tragic figure of Ivan Chtcheglov who created the finest psychogeographical work – his 1953 essay *Formulary for a New Urbanism*.[11] Chtcheglov's text is still the most useful 'manual' for an experimental drift through an ambient location and one that we could use on Merseyside. In the essay he begins by lamenting the Paris that is now lost (to urban development) and decrying the current 'boredom' of the city. Through aimlessly wandering, Chtcheglov finds solace in the strange place names of Parisian features:

Hotel of Strangers
Saint Anne Ambulance
Showerbath of the Patriarchs
Notre Dame Zoo
The swimming pool on the Street of Little Girls

These peculiar ambiences throw new light on the locations. 'Certain shifting angles, certain receding perspectives, allow us to glimpse original conceptions of space, but his vision remains fragmentary'. What are described are new perceptions of space, time and behaviour, all themes expressed in Lowry's writings. Chtcheglov, like Lowry, draws on the atmospheric writings of the past in order to reinvent the present (Victor Hugo, Dumas, Poe). Chtcheglov considered the *dérive* akin to a form of psychoanalysis and 'a good replacement for a mass'. The paintings of Claude Lorrain evoke a 'perpetual invitation to voyage'. Lowry will have felt the same pull gazing out across the oceans.

The map is not the territory

Lowry's writing can be read as itself psychogeographic. Lowry takes the 'map' of a location, documenting and poetically reworking the experience of individuals drifting through that terrain. For chapter ten of *Under The Volcano* Lowry took a Mexican cantina menu and reproduced it in the narrative of the novel, using its

---

9   Clarisse Francillon, 'My Friend Malcolm', in *Malcolm Lowry: Psalms and Songs*, ed. Margerie Lowry (New York: Plume Books, 1975), p. 88.
10 Francillon, 'My Friend Malcolm', p. 96.
11 Gilles Ivain (Ivan Chtcheglov), 'Formulary for a New Urbanism', in Andreotti and Costa (eds.), *Theory of the Dérive*, pp. 14–17.

mistranslations to spring off into other fields of expression and suggestion. The accidental, experiential nature of the object here is important; it is no longer a cartography but a poetic terrain. In 1957 Debord took a map of Paris and cut it up, collaging it back into a new ensemble called *The Naked City* (heralding, incidentally, the Situationist technique of *détournement*). Again, the original meaning of the object is forgotten or overwritten by new meaning. Lowry's use of quotations and references, while causing him much anguish because of his fear of being accused of plagiarism (especially in relation to Conrad Aiken and Nordahl Grieg), was echoed in his protégé David Markson's novel *Reader's Block*. If only Lowry had been aware (perhaps he was?) of Lautréamont's dictum, much beloved of the Surrealists and Situationists: 'Plagiarism is necessary [...] it clasps an author's sentence tight, uses his expressions, eliminates a false idea, replaces it with the right idea'.[12]

The patterns evident in life and the natural world could be utilised in artistic expression. Lowry's famous letter to Jonathan Cape justifying the form of the manuscript for *Under the Volcano* and arguing the case for it to be published as it stands reads like a journey or a walk through the terrain of a great artistic sensibility. The 'subject' (ostensibly the publisher, Cape, but subsequently the reader) is guided through the novel by Lowry but is invited to reflect and drift. He speaks of the reader at the beginning of the novel thinking '*God, this is tough going*' but being driven on by 'reports which had already reached his ears of the rewarding vistas further on'. 'The first chapter [...] sets [...] the mood and tone of the book as well as the slow melancholy tragic rhythm of Mexico itself – its sadness – and above all else establishes the *terrain*'.[13] The author leads the reader through the pages and the place, acknowledging that along the way he or she will discover ceaseless wonders.

Much has been written about Lowry's fascination with the occult and the appearance of cabbalistic imagery in his works. This too, I would argue, has a psychogeographical aspect to it. Critics (especially literary ones) tend to be dismissive of Lowry's enthusiasm for the work of Charles Fort, G. I. Gurdjieff and P. D. Ouspensky. Yet Ouspensky's creation (or adoption, depending on which account you favour) of the 'Fourth Dimension' in *Tertium Organum* echoes aspects of the *dérive*. In his work Ouspensky was interested in accounting for a new order of experience, the myriad thoughts and experiences incomprehensible to the usual human way of viewing phenomena. Lowry (and the psychogeographers) sought to explore though physical and textual drifting a variant of such a vision. The 'passage of a few people through a brief moment in time' suggests an Ouspenskian mode: 'The true motion which lies at the basis of everything is the motion of thought'.[14]

Quoting Katherine Mansfield (herself a devotee of Gurdjieff), Lowry states, 'Major literature, in short, is an initiation into truth'.[15] For Lowry the cabbala was 'a system

---

12   Comte de Lautréamont, *Maldoror and Poems* (Harmondsworth: Penguin, 2006), p. 274.
13   Letter to Jonathan Cape, in *Selected Letters*, p. 58.
14   P. D. Ouspensky, *Tertium Organum: The Third Canon of Thought / A Key to the Enigmas of the World* (London: Routledge and Kegan Paul, 1981), p. 290.
15   'Work in Progress', *The Malcolm Lowry Review*, 21/22 (1988), p. 99.

of thought that creates a magical world within this one'. Lowry was also influenced by W. B. Yeats' esoteric concept of the 'physical-psychic experience' (Lowry called it the 'single psychic experience'). Yeats' book *A Vision* combines anecdote, automatic writing, observation and occult speculation. It is a difficult book with an unusual, confusing and ornate form (Lowry described his own work as having a 'churrigueresque' structure) and is obscure in much the same way that Lowry's texts, borrowing heavily from Yeats – especially the symbolic image of the 'wheel' – would be criticised for being. (Interestingly, a hypertext companion to *A Vision* is available on the internet with the intention of making the work more accessible and easy to navigate [http://www.yeatsvision.com]. One wonders whether a similar project might be useful for Lowry's works, making a 'drift' through the text a 'virtual' possibility.)

For Yeats the phantasmagoria is defined as a shifting series of real or imaginary figures as seen in a dream or *created as an effect in a film*. This theme is echoed in the articulations of the importance of 'glimpsed phenomena' evident in early writings on psychogeography. The borders of the mind, like those of the landscape, are constantly shifting and blurring. And so any trek around a landscape such as the Wirral shifts and blurs, changes focus; its form is transformed by the sea mist, by the destructive imposition of architecture (the ventilation shafts of the Mersey Tunnel; a lighthouse) and by mind-altering substances. Recurring symbols, whether they be in poetry, stories or a landscape, are to the psychogeographical imagination bearers of meaning and cohesion.

Leys and 'the Leys': psychogeography, Liverpool and Cuernavaca

Undertaking his own *dérive* through the life and works of Gustave Flaubert, Julian Barnes asks: 'Why does the writing make us chase the writer... Why aren't the books enough?'[16] Barnes is intrigued by two of Flaubert's 'unfinished books' in much the same way that Lowry scholars obsess over his mostly unfinished *oeuvre*. Lowry admired Flaubert (Markson describes *Madame Bovary* as one of Lowry's 'big books'[17]) and there are parallels between the two writers. Like Flaubert, Lowry couches his complaints in 'letters of astonishing fluency'. Flaubert came to resent the success of *Madame Bovary*, his masterpiece, which 'makes others see him as a one-book author'.[18] The kind of exercise that Barnes undertakes can be very effective – drifting through the detritus of a writer's life and works, making one's own 'sense' of the fragments collected along the way. With Lowry it is also useful to take a 'physical' trip around his work and early life and this is what the walk is all about. In *Rings of Saturn*, the German writer W. G. Sebald undertook a walking tour of the Suffolk coast, spinning off from his supposed route into history, memory, art and death, and this could serve as an inspiration for the Wirral experience. But what might we find on such an excursion?

---

16 Julian Barnes, *Flaubert's Parrot* (London: Picador, 1985), p. 2.
17 David Markson, *Malcolm Lowry's Volcano: Myth, Symbol and Meaning* (New York: Times Books, 1978), p. 230.
18 Barnes, *Flaubert's Parrot*, p. 25.

The undertaking of a psychogeographic walk around Lowry's Wirral (rather than Mexico) is not as perverse as it first seems. As Janet and Colin Bord note in their book *Mysterious Britain*, the Wirral is one of the areas of the UK not yet fully explored for its zodiac mirrored trackways and leys. It is suspected that a formation of ley lines occurs on this site and it would be useful for any Lowry excursion around the location to bear this unusual aspect in mind (one aspect of the psychogeographic approach is to follow randomly selected/composed routes). Lowry would approve of such a mystical component to his birthplace, aside from the obvious attraction of linking the name of his former public school (The Leys) with the 'old straight tracks'. As Debord did with his *Naked City* map, we can take the terrain apart and create our own new route(s) through and around the locations of Lowry's past. In addition, the psychogeographical offers the possibility of imbuing existing places with new meanings. 'Lowry Bank', for example, is a location spotted on a recent drift across the terrain. Scenes such as this offer great psychogeographic potential. Beyond 'Lowry Bank' is the river Mersey, and the route out to the sea was crucial for Lowry. The most satisfying drift around the Wirral keeps close to the water or to points along the route at which, even if the sea is not visible, its presence is felt. The Hoylake golf course, home to 'Hell Bunker', is a good example of this, where the tranquillity and staidness of the golf course and its clubhouse are haunted by the sea waves beyond. It's impossible not to imagine the young Lowry driving his golf balls across the green but dreaming of the vast indifferent ocean and what it holds for the intrepid traveller. Lowry's works were born of sea and tragically died in flames.

Using the principles of psychogeographical techniques, is it possible to find, for example, Cuernavaca on Merseyside? Debord's 'Exercise in Psychogeography' (*Potlach #2*) or 'Introduction to a Critique of Urban Geography' offer such possibilities. In the latter piece Debord relates the anecdote of a friend who 'wandered though the Harz region of Germany while blindly following the directions of a map of London'. The former essay advocates the collecting of aphorisms/place names/characters and twisting them into surprising new formations ('Claude Lorrain is psycho-geographical in the juxtaposition of a palace neighbourhood and the sea'[19]). In any case, Lowry himself suggests such a methodology. Chris Ackerley and Lawrence Clipper note how Lowry drew on Melville's *Redburn* for inspiration, the young hero of that text adopting an antiquated map of Liverpool to help him navigate the city.[20] Rumney once set out to record a *dérive* around Venice that resulted in the work 'The Leaning Tower of Venice'. The images augment the text to exhibit and recreate the various sites of interest. Of course these images are not usually the 'conventional' tourist view of the city but are trained instead on the hidden aspects of the location.

---

19   Guy Debord, 'Exercise in Psychogeography', in Andreotti and Costa (eds.), *Theory of the Dérive*, p. 42.
20   Chris Ackerley and Lawrence J. Clipper, *A Companion to Under the Volcano* (Vancouver: University of British Columbia Press, 1984), p. 362.

Top: Hell Bunker. Middle: Lowry Bank, Seacombe
Bottom: view of the Mersey from Lowry Bank with the Liverpool skyline

Photos by Colin Dilnot

Conclusion

The conditions of the theory of psychogeography are inherent in the work of Malcolm Lowry. Psychogeography involves a rejection of the usual motives for movement and action, instead embracing 'the drift', but at the same time calculation and recording of the possibilities of such a *dérive*. I believe that to some extent this is how Lowry worked: he let his poetic sensibilities flow, creating a mesmerising terrain of linguistic play. Yet at the same time he was careful to record everything and shape it into a textual piece capable of being fixed and read by another individual. It was once said of Ralph Rumney that he believed the production of artefacts to be valueless 'unless it is born out of a firm and consistent philosophy of life'. Lowry did not manage to complete his 'Voyage that Never Ends'; nor perhaps should he have. As Chtcheglov noted years ago (and as a psychogeography of 'that terrible city whose main street is the ocean' confirms): 'dreams spring from reality and are realised in it'.[21] Despite Lowry's wish 'alternately to kill Liverpool and myself',[22] the landscape and the ghosts of his past are still there.

> My imagination leads me to visualise a sort of battle between life and delirium, in which life [...] is fighting to give that delirium a form, a meaning.[23]

---

21   Chtcheglov, 'Formulary for a New Urbanism', p. 15.
22   *Selected Letters*, p. 8.
23   Lowry, 'Work in Progress', p. 74.

WESTERN UNION
(THE WESTERN UNION TELEGRAPH COMPANY)
CABLEGRAM

ANGLO-AMERICAN TELEGRAPH Co., Ld.   CANADIAN NATIONAL TELEGRAPHS.

RECEIVED AT YORKSHIRE HOUSE, CHAPEL STREET, LIVERPOOL, 3. (Tel. No. Central, 2274.)

BSE 219 MEXICOCITY 26 5

1938 AUG 6 A 2 15 g

NLT AYRCLIFF   39   AYRTON & ALDERSON SMITH
        LPOOL   10 DALE ST

MUCH REGRET INABILITY RECOMMEND AGENT STOP SUGGEST REQUESTING

INTERVENTION BRITISH CONSUL LOSANGELES AUGUST ALLOWANCE ARRIVED AFTE

MALCOMS DEPARTURE SHALL APPRECIATE YOUR INSTRUCTIONS

                                LEYHAM

FORM NO. 6.

WESTERN UNION
(THE WESTERN UNION TELEGRAPH COMPANY)
CABLEGRAM

79

ANGLO-AMERICAN TELEGRAPH Co., Ld.   CANADIAN NATIONAL TELEGRAPHS.

RECEIVED AT YORKSHIRE HOUSE, CHAPEL STREET, LIVERPOOL, 3. (Tel. No. Central, 2274.)

JT 38 LOSANGELES CALIF 98 1/43 10/821P   3 AUG 11 AM 6 28

AYRCLIFF LPOOL   79   AYRTON AND ALDERSON SMITH
                                10 DALE ST.

MALCOLM IN DEPLORABLE PHYSICAL MENTAL CONDITION RESULT CONTINUOUS

EXCESSIVE DRINKING MOVED HIM TO SEASHORE UNDER SUPERVISION TO SUPPLY

FOOD AND CUT LIQUOR CONSUMPTION MAXIMUM ONE QUART DAILY UNABLE REDUCE

THIS AMOUNT WITHOUT HOSPITALIZATION TEMPORARILY SEPARATED WIFE WHO WORKS

SMALL SALARY RECOMMEND

(THE WESTERN UNION TELEGRAPH COMPANY)

CABLEGRAM

ANGLO-AMERICAN TELEGRAPH Co., Ld.   CANADIAN NATIONAL TELEGRAPHS.

RECEIVED AT YORKSHIRE HOUSE, CHAPEL STREET, LIVERPOOL, 3. (Tel. No. Central, 2274.)

2VAJASL122 LOSANGELESCALIF 76 1/35 14

NLT AYRCLIFFE   23   AYRTON AND ALDERSON SMITH
                                10 DALE ST.
                    LPOOL

MALCOLM ENTERED SANATORIUM SATURDAY ACCORDANCE DOCTORS RECOMMENDATION

DESPITE WIFES REFUSAL COOPERATION UNLESS I AGREED SEND MALCOLM TO

MENNINGER PSYCHOANALYTIC SANATORIUM TOPEKA KANSAS IMMEDIATELY STOP

CONFERRED PSYCHOANALYST THREE YEARS MENNINGER STAFF/HE STATES

FORM No. 6.

WESTERN UNION

(THE WESTERN UNION TELEGRAPH COMPANY)
INCORPORATED IN THE STATE OF NEW YORK, U.S.A., WITH LIMITED LIABILITY.

CABLEGRAM

ANGLO-AMERICAN TELEGRAPH Co., Ld.   CANADIAN NATIONAL TELEGRAPHS.

RECEIVED AT YORKSHIRE HOUSE, CHAPEL STREET, LIVERPOOL, 3. (Tel. No. Central, 2274.)

BSE 12 LOSANGELES CALIF 136 1/41 15TH

                                AYRTON AND ALDERSON SMITH
NLT AYRCLIFF LPOOL   110   10 DALE ST.

MALCOLMS WIFE SUED FOR DIVORCE ASKING ALIMONY SET FOR HEARING AUGUST

AUGUST EIGHTH FINALLY OBTAINED CONTINUANCE OF HEARING TO THIRTIETH

THIS DELAYED DEPARTURE UNTIL JULY TWENTYSIXTH MADE EXTREMELY

SATISFACTORY AND BENEFICIAL ARRANGEMENT MALCOLM SATISFIED AND

BELIEVE FATHER WILL BE

Label from Mezcal Del Consul bottle

No se puede vivir sin amar

Ailsa Cox

Where are the letters you wrote? The letters you wrote, the first week of term, *no se puede vivir sin amar*, and her face in the margin – a scribble of curls, the biro punching holes for eyes – where did they go? – those mad letters – folded flat between the pages of Eliot and Donne and the Complete Works of Shakespeare. *Come back to me, just for one day.*

Where is she? Madeleine – on a hilltop just outside Lancaster, in a celestial city made from clean, geometrical blocks. She fought hard to get here, and the habit of work has become so engrained, she reads every book that she's studying twice.

> *Overlooking one of these valleys, which is dominated by two volcanoes, lies, six thousand feet above sea level, the town of* – how do you say it? – *Quauhnahuac.*

Where are the letters? You didn't know the address, and don't even think about asking her parents – *don't touch her, don't ever come near her again* – all you knew was the name of the university. But those crumpled pages got to her eventually, although you don't know that, because you never check your pigeonhole for the answer you never expected. You don't leave this room often. Stopped going to lectures. Not that you ever had serious intentions of ever becoming a teacher. You're at college because you thought there'd be a wider choice of drugs, and there are, though you have to travel to Bradford to get them.

You don't know she's on her way, a tiny figure swamped in her army surplus greatcoat, long skirts already damp with slush. She speeds down the Spine between colleges, pushing against the wind funnelled down from the Irish Sea, past the film soc flyers and concert posters and the guys from the Socialist Workers and the International Marxists thrusting leaflets at her, the squared-off fists and the hammers and chains, the pigs in top hats, *Boycott Barclays*. She dips her gaze when she sees someone she knows – there are just too many faces – and besides, Madeleine's shy. She knows how to make friends but not how to keep them. Her head hums with music. Fairport Convention.

> *So Janet tied her kirtle green a bit above her knee*
> *And she's gone to Carterhaugh as fast as go can she*

She crosses Alex Square and leaves the main campus by a side-exit, hurrying towards the hitching point, where half a dozen other students are already standing by the roadside, heading for town to do their shopping. All the cars are going to town. They clamber into rattling Citroëns, Fords and Morris Minors, two by two, and three and four, till the first lot of hitchers have disappeared, and another half dozen taken their place. Every time a door opens, Madeleine shakes her head again. Wrong direction. Should have advertised for a lift, shouldn't leave it all to chance. But that's Madeleine for you. She doesn't think straight. *She's gone to Carterhaugh as fast as go can she.*

Why not just ring, let him know that she's coming? Impossible. Such thoughts never crossed her mind; these are the days when, for some, telephones are foreign objects. Madeleine's parents don't have a phone, and that's why she's promised to write home every Sunday; but she won't tell them what she's up to this weekend. She won't tell a soul.

Madeleine's come straight from childhood. Before she left, her mother gave instructions – how to iron clothes, how to boil an egg – and her father laid down a strict warning against all those things she had in fact tried; but so far as most practicalities are concerned, she's as helpless as a puppet newly summoned into life. It's hard to imagine how clueless she is, and how innocent; how much she lives in the world of books, more at home in Hardy's Wessex than with the ground beneath her feet; how hazy her sense of direction. Wandering dreamily down the dim corridors in the Hall of Residence, she sometimes completes several circuits before she stops at the door to her room.

At each corner, a glass box where the students cook and eat, and sit on the low windowsills at night, swapping stories about ghosts. There's a pale-lashed redhead who lives on boiled rice; and a self-absorbed couple who clatter back and forth with saucepans; and then there's Gilbert, the ex-seaman, who prides himself on his rationalism – '*Transactional analysis!* That is the answer, I am telling you. Here in this book – *transactional analysis,* my friend!' And there's Josh, the American – *my parents are Italian* – small and darkly apelike, but so open and without subterfuge, she sometimes wonders if she's misread his intentions.

The darkness behind the glass covers the Lancashire hills and pastures, the Lune estuary, the shifting sands of Morecambe Bay, and then the Lakes, all of these places a mystery to a girl newly transplanted from Walsall. (Josh thought she meant *Warsaw – so you're from Poland?*) Silverdale, Hesketh Bank, Torrisholme – and then over in Yorkshire other small galaxies – Bingley, Shipley, Keighley, names on the torn-out map that he sent with the letters. The map that's in her coat pocket, with the *Boycott Barclays* leaflet.

* * *

Ten to one, not a bad ratio, but most of the chicks are all one and the same, into glam rock or Motown or some other Radio One type of crap. He's bored with them already, fucking tired of listening to their little rodent squeals. That's why he started thinking about Madeleine again, he was sorry for walking away from her, he shouldn't have just let her go. He could see her like she was in the room – the white centre parting cutting a track through the dark mass of hair – shouldn't have done, but what else could he do? He was listening to *Astral Weeks* again, *say goodbye, goodbye, goodbye…* that was probably what did it, and the Manali lighting a space in his skull. Lighting a space, and he saw them walking the long road home when the last bus had gone. He wanted her badly – so much that it hurt – *Don't do this to me Maddie* – but he never said he loved her. Never talked that kind of shit.

His name's Peter Sugden. PS. His mates from school – Mike Wells (Smells), Martin Fry (Eggsie) – call him Snug, and so does everyone back home, except for his Nan, but it's like a kid's name, so at college he's an ordinary Pete.

DISCO!!!!

FRIDAY NITE

FRESHERS BALL

A red-cheeked woman in a mob cap, the white uniform glazed by the surgical lights of the empty canteen.

'We're closing, son.'

The juice-machine sluicing back and forth and back...

'We're closing.'

...and forth again.

'I can do you a few chips?'

Rattling the empty metal coffins where they keep the vegetables.

'Are you not going to the disco?'

MARC BOLAN!

BOWIE!

ROXY MUSIC!!!

'I hate discos.'

He picks up a book someone's left by the till. Greyish, elephantine figures on the cover; the bottom corner bent and curled.

'Was it you left it here?'

'Yes,' he lies.

He eats the chips with his fingers, smearing ketchup on the pages as he flips through at random, the dense print seething like ants. *'Mescal,' said the Consul* – that catches his attention – someone has underlined passages – *no se puede vivir sin amar*. He mouths the words; he likes the sounds – *amas amat amatis amant* – *Thus spake the Sybil of Cumae* – *he's bright but he's lazy* – white light, a clear space in his head. That little man boiling with fury – *get off, don't you touch her, don't ever come near...* Thought he was going to take a swing at him... Like he knew, like he could smell the spunk on her. Madeleine.

The Perspex cube continues its slow waltz, back and forth, the juice a luminous orange – you shouldn't have let her go like that, serves you right if you're miserable, what if I am – and then he knows what to do. Yes, write, speak to her, now. He's never felt lighter, as he leaves the canteen, the book jammed in his pocket, so weightless he's floating like a balloon, a bright orange balloon drifting high in the clouds.

* * *

Finally, she decides to walk down the hill from Bailrigg, and try her luck on the main road. She's damp through to her skin, her nose pinched with cold – almost changing her mind, when the Morris van stops. 'I'm going so far as Garstang,' the driver says, in his gruff Lancashire voice. 'I can drop you off at Forton Services, if that's any good.'

She squeezes into the front, minding her feet like he tells her. The back's stuffed with oil cans and bits of old timber.

'Your best bet's the A65, if you're making for Yorkshire, head back towards Kirkby Lonsdale, that's what I'd do.'

In just a few minutes, she's at Forton Services, trying to catch the attention of any drivers going towards Kirkby Lonsdale.

Come back to me – pages and pages, A4 narrow feint, some of them crumpled, like they'd been thrown away and rescued – the thick blue writing looping over the lines, the curling tails of the g's and y's, the rounded arches in the way he wrote M's, like church windows. *Madeline* spelt wrongly. She knew it was him. *Come back to me* – but she never left. He did.

She tried to explain, but her dad just kept shouting: *Get off. Don't you touch her.* Right there in the street, with the car engine running.

A shrug of his shoulders, and Snug disappeared. That's what he did – went off without a word. She kept watch for him all summer, into winter and spring – looking out for the long-limbed prowl and mocking glance.

Don't ever come near her again.

'Your doctor back home has phased out the Librium, which is good, we don't want any dependency, but I want you to promise me that if you have any problems, if you feel at all depressed, you'll make an appointment to see me.'

Madeleine nods politely but she doesn't really understand why she's been called in. That story's over; it happened to somebody else.

And yet when the letters arrive, bundled together in an elastic band, she feels a stab in her heart, and when she reads those words, *no se puede vivir sin amar,* her head reels like she's been drinking. She doesn't make her mind up right away. She has lectures to go to, and also Josh has written a play and he thinks she might like to audition... But later that night she uncreases the letters and reads them again, trying to decipher the sections where the writing gets smaller or larger, the loops closing up or widening like lasso's, coming back again and again to that phrase, *no se puede vivir,* and she knows that it's true. She's been given a sign. And the story starts over again.

After Kirkby Lonsdale, it isn't so bad. The lifts come easily, though it gradually dawns on Madeleine that she's taking the long way, and the place that in her head is so many miles distant isn't as far from Lancaster as she first imagined. She's been travelling for hours, chattering away in return for the ride – that's why the drivers pick her up, for conversation – and she's glad of the silence, sitting high in the cab, invulnerable above the streams of traffic. The lorry driver seems old to her, as old as her dad, though, if she knew it, he thinks he's young – thirty-seven – and like her dad he's taciturn. He smells of Juicy Fruit. The pale hairs curl round his metal watchband.

Remember, remember – the pyres made of twigs and old planks, smashed chairs and bookcases – *gunpowder, treason and plot.* In the darkness, she makes out the constellations of towns and factories lining the moors. *Gargrave, Skipton, Barnoldswick.* Place names flip past like playing cards. *Put a tiger in your tank.*

'Five minutes,' he says, pulling up by the side of a transport café. All she's eaten today is an apple, but she's too well-mannered to let the driver treat her, staying in the cab reading, snug in her big coat, the map, yes, still in her pocket. Kids are hanging round the entrance with a guy made from cushions, no head she can see, just a trilby tipped on his chest, like he's sleeping it off.

> *And the earth itself still turning on its axis and revolving around that sun, the sun revolving around the luminous wheel...*

'Is it good?' says the driver, snatching the grey paperback. 'What is it, horror story?'

'No, not really.'

He settles himself into his seat and releases the brake, his big freckled arm flexing. It seems he wants entertaining after all, so she tells him about her family, and what she's studying at university, and everything she's told the other strangers she's met on her journey. She's going to see a friend, she says.

'Not your boyfriend?'

For a second she thinks he's sizing her up – but no, she's wrong, because, in the next instant, he's handed her a wallet with pictures. A wife, two kids and a three-legged dog. He says he'll take her right to the college; be there in no time. It's not far off his route, it's no hardship.

So Madeleine why are you scared? She is not.

> *I forbid you maidens all that wear gold in your hair*
> *To travel to Carterhaugh, for young Tam Lin is there.*

He's being kind to her, paternal like the doctor. *Promise... if you have any problems...*

'It's one of them places, not far from the town, but it's awkward like. You have to know it.'

They've left the main road. The big lorry, so smooth up to now, suddenly lurches and stutters. Turning a sharp corner, it rubs up against a row of cottages, close enough to startle the cats in the living room windows.

'It's okay,' she says, 'I think I know where I am.'

She's scared because she's going to be sick. She can't breathe for the smell of Juicy Fruit.

'Thanks,' she says, 'I can find my own way. I don't want to put you to any trouble.'

'It's a pleasure.'

He strokes her knee. He pats her leg. He touches her knee, only a knee, but still there's something in his face, in the satisfied purr of the masculine voice.

'Can you let me out please?' she asks, very politely.

'There's no stopping here. No pedestrians.'

No stopping. Her hand on the door. She looks straight at him and repeats, 'Let me out.'

'What's up with thee lass? What's to do?'

> *...the world itself was bursting, bursting into black spouts of villages catapulted into space, with himself falling through it all...*

'We're there,' he says, 'right after these lights.'

> *...falling, into a forest, falling –*

Hand on the door, on the catch. 'Let me out.'

* * *

Where are the letters you wrote? Sometimes a thought skims your mind as you put a match to the sweet Manali black – *no se puede* – already scenting the clean Himalayan air – *no se puede vivir sin amar* – the words playing like notes from a tune. They are words, they are feelings, they fade and return. *Come back to me, just for one day.* And what if she did? What if, even now, she was walking through the gloomy Victorian college, wrapped in her oversized coat, the dark scribble of hair smelling of bonfires? Ah Madeline, sweetheart, forgive me! What if she knocked on the door?

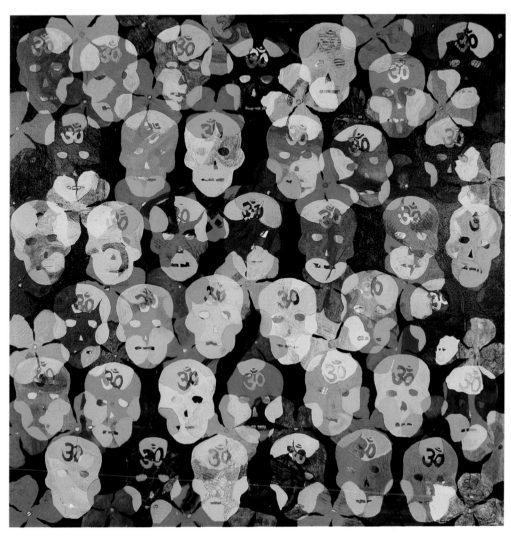

Pete Flowers, *Skulls and Flowers – Las Calaveras y las Flores*, 2008,
oil on canvas, 80 x 80 cm

Collection of the Artist

Pete Flowers, *Skeleton Angels – Los Esqueletos Angelicos*, 2008,
oil on canvas, 80 x 80cm

Collection of the Artist

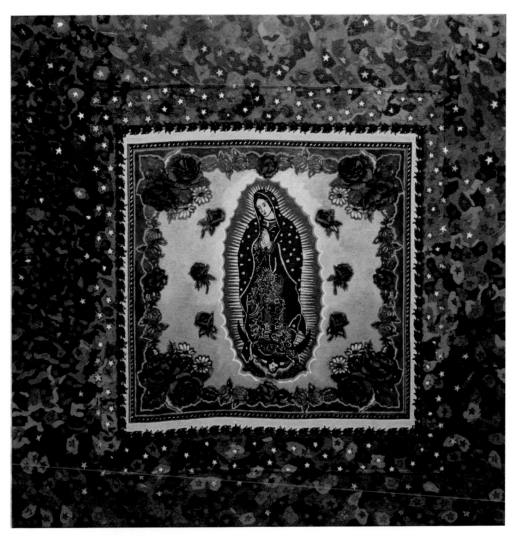

Pete Flowers, *Prayer for Consul*, 2009,
oil on canvas, 80 x 80 cm

Collection of the Artist

Lowry holding a bottle of Bols dry gin and a paperback, Dollarton, 1953

University of British Columbia Library, Rare Books and Special Collections,
Malcolm Lowry Collection, BC 1614/107

'Eridanus, Liverpool':
echoes and transformations at the edge of eternity

Annick Drösdal-Levillain

> ...the common occurrence of rain falling into the sea. So terrible and foreign
> to the earth has this world become that a child may be born into its Liverpools
> and never find a single person any longer who will think it worth pointing out
> to him the simple beauty of a thing like that.[1]

Malcolm Lowry

'The Forest Path to the Spring' is the last piece Lowry worked on before his death,
and it is also the last story of the posthumously edited collection *Hear Us O Lord
from Heaven Thy Dwelling Place*. It holds treasures to be unveiled by a reader willing to
lend a 'floating ear'[2] to its echoes and tintinnabulations, telling us about something
unnameable that is trying to get to the surface but can't come into the open, for
this would mean the death of the subject – as is foreseen by the story's narrator/
protagonist, who senses that he might well have vanished on the ever-shrinking
path to and from the spring.[3] I propose to explore 'The Forest Path to the Spring'
in the uncertain, oscillating twilight zone between zoom and focus, contraction
and expansion, attention and letting go, and to probe the deep-running metaphoric
undercurrents which ballast Lowry's poetic prose, to finally take a sip of that subtle
transformative 'psycho-poethic' cocktail blending past and present, individual and
universal dimensions, with a touch of Mersey stretching towards the Isle of Man[4] – a
certain sense of humanity is at stake – thanks to the omnipresent references to the
Manx fisherman's hymn harbouring the collection. The small community of Eridanus
is gathered around a Manx hymn-singing ideal father-figure – Quaggan, the Manx
boat-builder, 'whose boat shed was large as a small church' (p. 222) and who 'seemed
to be the father or grandfather of most of the other fishermen, so that, in the way of
Celts, it was a bit like a big family the entrance to which, for an outsider, I was to find
by no means easy' (p. 222).

---

1   'The Forest Path to the Spring', in *Hear Us O Lord from Heaven Thy Dwelling Place* (New York: Carroll & Graf, 1961), p.
     241.
2   A psychoanalytic rule defined by Sigmund Freud in 1912; the psychoanalyst should pay the same attention
     to everything that is being said by the patient, because the meaning of things heard often reveals itself in the
     aftermath.
3   'What if the path became shorter and shorter until I should disappear altogether one evening, when coming back
     with the water?' (p. 272).
4   Lowry spent ten days in the summer of 1919 on the Isle of Man with his brothers Wilfrid and Russell while their
     parents were on a business trip in India. We may see here a first happy form of exile not far from home. See Gordon
     Bowker, *Pursued by Furies: A Life of Malcolm Lowry* (New York: St Martin's Press, 1993), pp. 20–21.

103

Ringing circles

'The Bravest Boat', the first story of the collection, is launched to bring the reader through an ocean of stories of which 'Forest Path' is the coda. The toy boat seems to be meant to provide the reader with the minimal material to get through the expanding, interconnecting, ringing circles of the collection, and invites a plunge through several layers of meaning. Following the rippling effects of metonymies and metaphors chasing each other along Lowry's lines, the reader dives into abysmal depths, questioning 'the unfathomed deeps' (p. 20) the toy boat has over-sailed in pursuit of the riddling power of language at work under the artist's pen, to try to catch some of 'the underlying meaning of [his] symphony' (p. 283). Reading 'Forest Path', one has to go up and down and along the circles and layers of meaning of the text, metaphorically using the 'rotten old ladder'[5] (pp. 238, 264) salvaged on the beach and converted into steps by the narrator/protagonist, who realises that 'in converting both these derelicts [the ladder and a water cannister] to use I had prefigured something I should have done with my soul' (p. 282). Such recycling and transformation of 'derelicts' can be interpreted as a metaphor for Lowry's writing, constantly reusing bits and pieces of the past collected over the years in his little notebooks, in an attempt to 'transcend [the past] in the present' (p. 283).

Up and down and along, all this has to be more or less simultaneous and can be likened to the chain of signifiers – the 'verbal string'[6] – along which the signifieds branch off, opening new vistas. In 'Forest Path' at least three different signifieds, or 'offsprings', stem from the signifier 'spring' and pop lightly at the surface of the text: the source of water, the season, the source of life or birthplace: '*Eridanus*, Liverpool' (p. 226). Encrusted, almost fossil-like, in the body of the text, 'on the stern' (p. 226) of a wreck, the inscription leaves an indelible print of Lowry's origins, who carefully kept this 'source' (p. 226) alive thanks to the written word. A fourth variation creeps into the narrative when a hungry mountain lion, driven down to the forest by the snow, misses its 'spring' (p. 265) and virtually falls off the branch from which it was observing the praying narrator/prey on his meditative path back from the spring. On the next page, the verbal form playfully nudges the reader's ear as the narrator evokes his fear of something 'ready, on every side, to spring out of our paradise at us [...] ready to leap out and destroy me, to destroy us, and our happiness' (p. 266). But the lion is 'nothing so much as the embodiment in some frightful animal form of those nameless somnambulisms, guilts, ghouls of past delirium, wounds to other souls and lives, ghosts of actions approximating to murder, even if not my own actions in this life, betrayals of self and I know not what' (p. 266).

The repetition of the signifier 'spring' signals, as a sp/ringing bell would, that something is about to surface from the depths of the unconscious through the

---

5   Cf. Lowry's poem 'The Past': 'Like a rotten old ladder / [...] Up and down which / Each night my / Mind meaninglessly climbs'; in *Selected Poems of Malcolm Lowry*, ed. Earle Birney with the assistance of Margerie Lowry (San Francisco: City Lights Books, 1962), p. 69.

6   'La ficelle verbale'; an expression coined by Jacques Lacan in 1957.

porous surface of the literary text, which functions as a 'latticework'[7] set against the horror of the unnameable thing. Through this encounter with the lion, the narrator/protagonist/Lowry can 'name' fragments of 'that dark chaotic side of [him]self, [his] ferocious destructive ignorance' (p. 234). Such a playful variation on the signifier sends the reader/analyst on a trail of little 'chunks of jouissance' drifting among the flotsam of Lowry's prose. Something other can then flicker and dwindle, something unnameable but perceptible, recalling Joseph Conrad's aesthetic of writing: 'by the power of the written word to make you hear, to make you feel – it is, before all, to make you *see*'[8] and wrapping the reader in a 'liquescent'[9] rippling Lowryan echo-system.

A Lowryan echo-system of repetition and transformation

Ancient Chinese calligraphy is also called 'grass painting'[10] because the calligrapher is moving like grass in the wind. It is a form which shapes and perpetually reshapes itself in the return of the same. This is a rhythm which is not found in the flowing river but in the wash of the sea. And the rhythm can only be born when the artist 'is' what he is expressing, painting, playing, and at the same time can achieve the necessary distance to structure the encounter between inspiration and the repetitive movement, between high and low tide, in a stasis, an all-encompassing suspension, between the singular and the plural. The following extract provides a striking example of the sensory quality of Lowry's prose, with alliterations in /sh/, /s/ and /b/ miming the sound of the sea, the rhythmic ringing assonances in /i/, the metamorphosis of 'wash' into 'watch' taking us from 'hear' to 'see', while in between, we are made to 'feel' the lull of the waves with the /l/ sound:

> The *wash* from the *invisible* freighter, the *wash still invisible* itself from where we were on the path, could *be heard breaking all along* the curve of the beach as it approached us, and *simultaneously* it began, slowly at first, and gently, to rain, and as *the wash* of *undulating* silver *rippling into sight transversely spent itself against the rocks* we stopped to *watch* the rain like a *bead curtain falling behind a gap* in the trees, into the inlet below. (p. 285, emphasis mine)

The freighter slowly approaches, first 'invisible', then signalled by the repetitive beat of the wash. The alliterative /sh/ of the signifier 'wash' repeated three times is held in a ghostly suspension before it is allowed to ripple 'into sight' and spend itself 'against the rocks', letting the driftwood of the unconscious come to shore thanks to the artist's

---

7   Julia Kristeva expresses the double function of literature: 'a frail netting that is also a latticework, which, without protecting us from anything whatsoever, imprints itself within us, implicating us fully'; *Powers of Horror* (New York: Columbia University Press, 1982), p. 156.

8   Joseph Conrad, 'Preface' to *The Nigger of the 'Narcissus'* (London: Dent, 1897), p. xxvi.

9   The windows of the shack are 'liquescent on the floor' (p. 261).

10 See Henri Maldiney, 'L'Esthétique des rythmes' (1967), in *Regard, Parole, Espace* (Lausanne: L'Age d'Homme, 1973), pp. 147–72.

loving, somehow careless care. The signifiers lightly pop up as if out of a whirlpool,[11] or perhaps should we say a Liverpool?

There is a Taoist quality to the way landscapes are depicted in 'Forest Path'. A 'platinum circle of sun' (p. 240) recurs throughout the narrative; silhouetted in it are the pine trees which 'at night [...]would write a Chinese poem on the moon' (p. 216), later transmuted by the narrator's vision into an armada of windjammers ablaze – 'a whole blazing Birkenhead Brocklebank dockside of fiery Herzogin Ceciles' (p. 259) – emerging straight from misty Merseyside sights of majestic windjammers such as the *Herzogin Cecilie*,[12] remnant of a disappearing world engulfed by steam, industrialisation and war, but transfigured and somehow salvaged by this powerful evocation. The sad and sordid wreckage of this ship in 1936 off the coast of Devon[13] is not without an echo of Lowry's own sorry end some twenty years later in East Sussex.

This passage concentrates several layers of references to Lowry's Mersey background, all of which hover between the heroic and the tragic. The Birkenhead docks had long been prosperous and industrious, but a disaster hit those docks on 6 March 1909,[14] four months before Lowry's birth. The breaking, clanking sounds of 'a whole blazing Birkenhead Brocklebank dockside of fiery Herzogin Ceciles' are re-echoed in a description of the tidal storm hurling itself in 'elemental despair' (p. 255) against the shack, 'the sound of ruination' (p. 255) hammering at the piles with 'wild elemental menace' (p. 255), 'horrible commotions of logs, jarring thunders dithering the whole little shack so that the lamp brackets rattled with the windows' (p. 255) in a hellish

---

11 See also 'Whirlpool' (*Selected Poems*, p. 65). The poem chimes with Lowry's poetic prose, casting the echo further over the 'Lowryscape'.

12 One of the last big sailing ships to roam the oceans, famous for winning the Grain Race several times. Lowry misspells the name as 'Cecile'.

13 'For seven weeks the *Herzogin Cecilie* lay stranded on the Hamstone whilst her four and a half thousand tons of grain rotted and fermented. The stench was appalling and fears of it polluting the beaches around Salcombe kept the owner and the local council arguing fit to bust. Every day huge crowds gathered to view the "Duchess" and local farmers made a fortune charging people to cross their land for a better look. Eventually the grain became so swollen that it started to crack the decks, and this seemed to galvanise the salvage attempts. By 7 June enough of her rotting cargo had been removed to allow the installation of powerful pumps, and on each high tide tugs repeatedly attempted to pull her off. At first it looked as if the "Duchess" was stuck fast, but finally, on 19 June the *Herzogin Cecilie* floated clear of the Hamstone. The local council still would not let her be towed into Salcombe, fearing all manner of disease, so in the end the "Duchess" was beached in Starhole Bay just at the entrance to the harbour. Unfortunately what appeared to be a "safe" sandy bottom, concealed rocks, and in the July gales she broke her back and her masts soon tumbled down into the sea. It was the beginning of the end. Ironically, if the Salcombe authorities had allowed her into harbour she would have been saved, unloaded and on her way long before the gales came. As it was the thing that the council feared most happened. The grain washed out of the wreck and fetched up on all the beaches. However, it didn't cause any pollution because the seagulls ate most of it, and the rest got washed away. So much for the experts. In the ensuing months all the fittings were stripped from the wreck, the beautiful figurehead sent to a museum in Finland, and the remains sold to a local scrap merchant for the princely sum of £225. A sorry end for a marvellous ship.' Peter Mitchell, www.submerged.co.uk (accessed March 2009).

14 Tom McCarthy gives a detailed account of this disaster in *Damburst: The Birkenhead Dock Disaster, March 6, 1909* (Birkenhead: Countyvise, 2006).

racket. We can hear the ghostly sounds of the Birkenhead disaster in the background.[15] *Birkenhead* is also the name of a famous ship whose wrecking off the coast of South Africa in 1852 initiated the emergency procedure of 'women and children first' known as the 'Birkenhead drill'.

It goes without saying that Lowry was intimate with disaster, and constantly hesitated between unattainable 'stars' and 'disaster' (literally, 'ill-starred'), drawing his strength like Martin Trumbaugh 'from the depths of the universe, from the depths among the stars, from the great world!'[16] Lowry once spelled this symptomatic signifier 'disastar', which, given his interest in the stars, rings a bell: 'I told my father in 1934 that there would be a war in the autumn of 1939, & he replied: "What kind of a son are you to tell his father & mother that the world is hurling to disastar?"'[17] One answer could be: a son or a 'starred subject' staring at the twinkling 'starry sky'[18] (p. 286) longing to become whole again, to rise like the mist evaporating in the sun, from the dark abysses of the mind towards the sky.[19]

In spite of Lowry's 'flight' away from Liverpool and the Wirral, images and impressions followed him, so that wherever he travelled, Liverpool surfaced in his prose,[20] revealing the 'love-hate'[21] relationship he entertained with 'that terrible city whose main street is the ocean' (p. 226) but whose 'sense of the sea and ships' surpasses even that of Curaçao.[22] Lowry's mother, whose maiden name was Boden, appears in an epic-poetic medallion: 'as if some ancient waterfront scene of conflagration in neighboring old windjammered Port Boden had been transported out of the past, in miniature, into the sky' (p. 260). 'Brocklebank' is another important signifier with a familiar ring for a

---

15 'An avalanche of timber and earth, swept forward by a gigantic wall of water, crashed down on the workmen, like the lid closing on a box. The wooden supports of the crane were smashed away by the onrushing wave and the huge machine was hurled into the water, turning the pit *into a hellish maelstrom* of broken timber and twisted metal. [...] On the dockside, other workers could only gape in stunned silence – too frozen by horror to utter a word. For an instant, the only sound that could be heard was the hissing of a broken steam pipe. Then men began running and shouting and the insistent shrill of a police whistle pierced the night'; McCarthy, *Damburst*, p. 6, emphasis mine.

16 'Through the Panama', in *Hear Us O Lord*, p. 34.

17 Letter to Margerie, Vancouver, September 1939, in *Sursum Corda! The Collected Letters of Malcolm Lowry, volume 1: 1926-1946*, ed. Sherrill E. Grace (Toronto: University of Toronto Press, 1995), p. 233.

18 Gordon Bowker points out another series of disasters which struck Lowry in 1912: first, Miss Bell, the boys' beloved nurse, left the Lowrys to work on a liner; then the *Titanic* disaster occurred on 15 April. Even as a three-year-old, Lowry cannot entirely have escaped the shock-wave (the ship was registered with the White Star Line in Liverpool, and Liverpool as a community was deeply shocked by the catastrophe). But this disaster may have led, indirectly, to Miss Bell's return. Bowker also quotes (*Pursued by Furies*, p. 10) a letter Miss Bell sent to Lowry for his third birthday in which she referred to Lowry's singing 'Twinkle, Twinkle Little Star' to her.

19 'Now, somewhere in the west where it was setting, the sun broke through the clouds, sending a flare of light across the water turning the rain into a sudden shower of pearls and touching the mountains, *where the mist rising from the black abysses fumed heavenward in pure white fire*' (p. 286, emphasis mine).

20 Liverpool is mentioned at some point in each story of *Hear Us O Lord*.

21 Tony Bareham points out that behind Lowry's Mexican and British-Columbian substance there is 'a reaction whose primary element is always England. To ignore this end of the process is like analyzing the nature of an echo without taking any account of the original source of the sound'; 'The Englishness of Malcolm Lowry', *The Journal of Commonwealth Literature*, 11.2 (1976), p. 135.

22 'The entrance to Curaçao is one of the most dramatic in the world. Hans Andersen would have loved the town. There is a more enormous sense of sea and ships in Curaçao than in any other part of the world I know of, except Liverpool'; 'Through the Panama', p. 68.

Mersey ear. Initially one of the world's biggest shipping companies, though beginning a slow decline in Lowry's days, it had its roots in Liverpool's heyday as a 'gateway to the world'. Thanks to a moon-shot medallion, the docks emerge from the mists of the past to be transfigured into 'an apparition of terrifying beauty' (p. 259) which turns out to be 'just the full moon rising clear of the pines behind the mountains' (p. 260). As the circular motif recurs 'like the back of a skull' (p. 240), it is transformed through an anamorphic process of displacement typical of the artistic gaze and central to Lowry's aesthetic. The poet's transfiguring vision is opposed to the materialistic and deadly touch of modern civilisation ('creator of deathscapes' [p. 279]), embodied by the sightseers whose preoccupation is to have the squatters evicted and sewers put in place: ' – WE NEED SEWERS NOT SYMPHONIES – ' (p. 276). The sewers sound like a jarring echo of the 'wooden backhouses of the little shacks', transfigured into 'monastic cells' (p. 217). Thus, the anti-poetic, disconnected, death-driven gaze of progress voiced by the city papers is denounced by the 'poet-seer', who states ironically that civilisation 'had not yet succeeded in hacking down the mountains and the stars' (p. 280). However, Lowry also strongly believed in the human capacity for redemption, for just as Burrard Inlet was able to cleanse itself of oil slicks, Lowry was able to recover from spectacular binges and downs.

The (S)hell oil refinery on the opposite bank of the inlet clearly embodies the activity of transformation of raw matter into a refined product at an industrial scale. Lowry's father was a cotton, sugar and oil broker, so he too was involved in the process of transformation – the very process that his 'disastrous' youngest son took up, but along less materialistic lines, transforming reality into prose, shuffling and reshuffling the debris of the past washed by the sea of the unconscious into the 'cave of his mind'.[23] The refinery itself is refined into a 'very fine' view and pun, that of a cathedral on fire: 'And undoubtedly the view in that specified direction is *very fine*, with the red votive candle of the burning oil wastes flickering ceaselessly all night before the gleaming open cathedral of the oil *refinery* –' (p. 227, emphasis mine). Lowry refines not only past memories but also language and meaning, as the unprophetic 'nonsense of love in a cottage' (p. 231) becomes a 'loving catchphrase' (p. 243).

Lowry, the all-round recycler

A language from beyond language, inhabited by the unconscious, filters through the cracks of Lowry's multi-layered text, merging Merseyside and British Columbia: sounds of the sea, sights of freighters coming and going, ringing bells, engines drumming to the beat of the universe enter the Eridanus chorus and inform this life 'on the very windrow of the world' (p. 232). It is as if Lowry had skipped from one edge, continent and ocean to another – from Liverpool, Europe, looking towards America over the Atlantic to Vancouver, Canada, looking towards Asia

---

23   'Resurgent sorrow is a sea in the cave / Of the mind – just as in the poem / It gluts it – though no nymphs will require a hymn; / [...] / Remorse, your host, who haunts the whirlpool where / The past's not washed up dead and black and dry / But whirls in its gulf forever, to no relief'; 'Whirlpool', p. 65.

over the Pacific. Centres have moved west to another north-western edge in similar surroundings, but on different scales. This change of scale corresponds to Lowry's tendency to dramatise reminiscences. The mountains of British Columbia, 'range beyond celestial range' (p. 216), are transformed onto a mythical scale to become 'the property of Titans', cloud-driven by 'Valkyries' (p. 216), in an echo of the Clwyd mountain range of North Wales visible from the Lowry home at Caldy. In the shift from one coast to the other, Lowry moved down the conventional social scale from a mansion such as Inglewood[24] to a squatter's shack. At the same time, he moved upwards on the spiritual path; he views himself as a 'poverty-stricken priest pacing in the aisles of a great cathedral at dusk' (p. 253) who still 'lacked spiritual equipment' (p. 282) but tried to make transformation ring along the 'Bell-Proteus path' (p. 257).[25]

The narrator/protagonist examining the structure of the cage-like foundations of his shack may be interpreted as Lowry endlessly revising his text, and revisiting the past. We have to bear in mind the specificity of Lowry's Mersey background, tightly linked to the transformations induced by ongoing industrialisation and modernity, for like many port cities, Liverpool counted many technological premières, ups and ensuing downs. Windjammers, railways, steamers, dams, canals, yards, locks and docks, all encapsulated in Lowry's metaphor of a 'celestial meccano' ('Through the Panama', p. 61), were part of this background on a personal and more general scale. With one eye still on nineteenth-century European industrialisation, Lowry observed and denounced the encroaching progress of modernity ('creating the moribund' [p. 280]) through the twentieth century. Awed by the dangers advancing civilisation held in its breast, sensing disaster at hand,[26] yet in a moving gesture of love, Lowry, the lover of language and nature, is 'overwhelmed' by 'the feeling of something that man had lost, of which these shacks and cabins, brave against the elements, but at the mercy of the destroyer, were the helpless yet stalwart symbol, of man's hunger and need for beauty, for the stars and the sunrise' (pp. 233-34). Lowry's beloved pier, 'disposed subaqueously in some ancient complex harmony of architectural beauty, an inverse moonlight geometry, beyond our conscious knowledge' (p. 256), stands for his transcended defiance of the Law, the Masters' discourse, the father's authority, social conventions and social discourse of linguists and grammarians, to which he pretended to be subjected, but from which he broke free. All this lies behind the oxymoronic simple-complex structure of the pier: 'It was simple and primitive. But what complexity must there have been in the thing itself, to withstand the elemental forces it had to withstand?' (p. 233).

---

24 Lowry's home at Caldy on the Wirral. The name 'Inglewood' appears in 'Forest Path' in a derisive remark about the names of the shacks on the beach: 'Is Inglewood a more imaginative name than Dunwoiken? Is Chequers? Or The White House?' (p. 220).

25 As noted above, Miss Bell was the beloved nurse in charge of the two youngest Lowry boys. Interestingly, the bell motif tends to recur in Lowry's prose, just like the stars.

26 This is echoed in *Lunar Caustic* by Bill Plantagenet's vision of the stars drifting towards universal disaster: 'The stars taking their places were wounds opening in his being, multiple duplications of that agony, of that eye. The constellations might have been monstrosities in the delirium of God. Disaster seemed smeared over the whole universe. It was as if he was living in the pre-existence of some unimaginable catastrophe'; *Lunar Caustic* (London: Jonathan Cape, 1977), pp. 20-21.

Lowry's capacity for moving from the individual to the universal emerges when the voice borders the primeval cry, or rather howl, recurring in the sonorous evocation of wolves howling 'from the mountains' (p. 216) as if they were tuning up to the wind 'wailing through the trees' (p. 216), to be ironically echoed by the train which tamely 'mooed like a cow' (p. 285). Progress has tamed the wild steam train and replaced it with 'a diesel engine of sinister appearance' (p. 285), just as it has unmanned the lighthouse, strapped a generator to its back and 'harnessed' the elements 'only for the earth's ruination and man's greed' (p. 241). The wailing train echoes beyond the limits of the story, along 'the great Cordilleras that ribbed the continent from Alaska to Cape Horn' (p. 230) towards Popocatepetl (p. 230) and *Under the Volcano*. Lowry's resistance to the modern world is inscribed in the metaphor of the train: all his life he stood in defiance of the modern world, which he felt would devour a man like him, not equipped for life among the 'creators of deathscapes', a man far too sensitive and 'porous', in a world where people cry out for sewers rather than symphonies. What is at stake is that lonely 'lamp of love' (p. 279) flickering in the echo-less snowstorms of a doomed humanity.

Was Lowry prophetic? Can we doubt it?

It seems that only from such a remote place, at 'the edge of eternity' (p. 279) or 'the very windrow of the world' (p. 232), could Lowry take in the world and give voice to that 'somethink *else* down there' (p. 254) which the diver has seen, frightening enough to keep him silent for two weeks while the thing 'rings': 'down, down, down you know, deep. [...] Migrations of a billion crabs, climbing all around him, migrating in the spring, aclambering around him, aswallering and stretching their muscles' (p. 254). In other words, this is the moment when the artist lets his own *lalangue* weave itself in the text – a language which, although personal, is at the same time universal, creating a sacred 'poethic' link to which the drifting, split but praying subject must cling[27] in a desperate attempt to order chaos, and transcend the past, so that the lighthouse can resume its 'beneficent signaling into the twilight' (p. 287). The encounter is possible in an '*Intermezzo*' (p. 231) where past and present can overlap, maps and shores merge in the twilight zone created by the poet in exile:[28] 'There is no poetry when you live there/ Those stones are yours those noises/ are your mind [...] But move you towards New Zealand or the Pole/ Those stones will blossom and the noises sing'.[29] Like a stray star, the poet sheds light on the ruins of language and civilisation, his gaze poised between the 'wild asters' (p. 229) and the constellations above, everlastingly bordering the blurred contours of the wrecked steamer of the 'defunct Astra Line' (p. 226) with its ghost-inscription: '*Eridanus*, Liverpool'.

---

27 'Dear Lord God, I earnestly pray you to help me order this work, ugly, chaotic and sinful though it may be, in a manner that is acceptable in Thy sight; [...] if my motives are obscure, and the notes scattered and often meaningless, please help me to order it, or I am lost' (p. 268).

28 'Exile is a form of suicide that may become rebirth'; Muriel Bradbrook, *Malcolm Lowry: His Art and Early Life, A Study in Transformation* (Cambridge: Cambridge University Press, 1974), p. 38.

29 'The Flowers of the Past', *Selected Poems*, p. 16.

The Birkenhead dock disaster, 1909

Ross Birrell and David Harding, *Cuernavaca: A Journey in Search of Malcolm Lowry*, 2006, commissioned by Kunsthalle Basel for the exhibition *Quauhnahuac: Die Gerade ist eine Utopie*, 1 October –12 November 2006

ABOVE: *You Like this Garden?*, installation shot, Kunsthalle Basel
Image: S. Burger, courtesy of Kunsthalle Basel

OPPOSITE TOP: *Cuernavaca: A Journey in Search of Malcolm Lowry*, film still
Courtesy of the Artists

OPPOSITE BOTTOM: *You Like This Garden?*, mural, Cuernavaca, 2006
Image: Hugh Watt

112

¿ LE GUSTA ESTE JARDIN ?
¿ QUE ES SUYO ?
¡ EVITE QUE SUS HIJOS LO DESTRUYAN !

WESTERN UNION
(THE WESTERN UNION TELEGRAPH COMPANY)
CABLEGRAM

ANGLO-AMERICAN TELEGRAPH Co., Ld.   CANADIAN NATIONAL TELEGRAPHS.

RECEIVED AT YORKSHIRE HOUSE, CHAPEL STREET, LIVERPOOL, 3. (Tel. No. Central, 2274.)

BJ LI1 LOSANGELESCALIF 48 6   1938 SEP 7 A 5 43

137   AYRTON & ALDERSON SMITH
                                    10 DALE ST.

NLT AYRCLIFF LPOOL

PSYCHOANALYSIS TEN DOLLARS HOUR HAVE ARRANGED FIVE HOURS

EXPECT KEEP SANITARIUM PENDING ADVICE STOP PRESENT AND CONTEMPLAT

EXPENSES EXCEED MONEY ON HAND SUGGEST ADDITIONAL FIVE HUNDRED

DOLLARS IMMEDIATELY MAILING ITEMIZED ACCOUNT STOP DOCTOR SUGGESTS

OUTDOOR PHYSICAL LABOR RANCH IF SON AGREEABLE WILL ENDEAVOR ARRAN

                              BENPARK

WESTERN UNION
(THE WESTERN UNION TELEGRAPH COMPANY)
CABLEGRAM

ANGLO-AMERICAN TELEGRAPH Co., Ld.   CANADIAN NATIONAL TELEGRAPHS.

RECEIVED AT YORKSHIRE HOUSE, CHAPEL STREET, LIVERPOOL, 3. (Tel. No. Central, 2274.)

1P AB 233 LOSANGELESCALIF 6TH 21

                                    1938 OCT 7 A 3 09

NLT AYRCLIFF   70   AYRTON AND ALDERSON SMITH

       LPL   10 DALE ST.

STATEMENT EXPENDITURES COMPLETE REPORT MAILED TWENTYEIGHTH

X SUGGEST CABLE FIVE HUNDRED DOLLARS SON BEHAVING FINE

WRITING EXERCISING SWIMMING

                              BENPARK

IGLO-AMERICAN TELEGRAPH Co. Ld.   CANADIAN NATIONAL TELEGRAPHS. 37

LOSANGELES CALIF 52 28   1959 SEP 29 A 4 37

YORKSHIRE HOUSE, ...E.. STREET, LIVERPOOL, 3. (Tel. No. Central, 2274.)

AYRTON AND ALDERSON SMITH LIVERPOOL

145

AVE FORWARDED COPY LETTER CAREY TWENTYFIFTH STATING MALCOLM

VED TWENTYSECOND SAME NIGHT PHONED SAYING GOING

ANGELES ABSENCE VERIFIED NEXT MORNING STATES NO MONEY FROM

BELIEVES RECEIVED FROM HOLLYWOOD MALCOLM NOT CONTACTED

BELIEVE GIRL BACKED MOVE SUGGEST NO FUNDS TO BREAK

OMANCE CABLE INSTRUCTIONS,

PARKS.

You may telephone us for a messenger

CLASS OF SERVICE DESIRED

DOMESTIC	CABLE
TELEGRAM	FULL RATE
DAY LETTER	DEFERRED
NIGHT MESSAGE	NIGHT LETTER
NIGHT LETTER	SHIP RADIOGRAM

Patrons should check class of service desired; otherwise message will be transmitted as a full-rate communication.

WESTERN UNION

1206-A

| CHECK |
| ACCT'G INFMN. |
| TIME FILED |

R. B. WHITE
PRESIDENT

NEWCOMB CARLTON
CHAIRMAN OF THE BOARD

J. C. WILLEVER
FIRST VICE-PRESIDENT

Send the following message, subject to the terms on back hereof, which are hereby agreed to

OCT 3 1939

Confirmation

NLT AYRTON & ALDERSON SMITH

LIVERPOOL ENGLAND

NEED OF MONEY CAUSED REAPPEARANCE VANCOUVER TWENTYEIGHTH VERY

DRUNK STATED IMMIGRATION OFFICIALS REFUSED ENTRY APPARENTLY

SPENT GIRLS MONEY DRINKING CAREY PLACING IN BOARDING HOME UNDER

SUPERVISION CARETAKER REFUSING FUNDS WHILE DRINKING   COPY

CAREYS LETTER FOLLOWING

PARKS

Cian Quayle, film still, 2009
Courtesy of the Artist

Uxorious prose: Malcolm Lowry's *October Ferry to Gabriola*

Nicholas Murray

Malcolm Lowry did what I wanted to do: he shipped from Liverpool on a freighter at the age of seventeen for an eighteen-month voyage to the Far East. He took a gap year before gap years were invented. The novel *Ultramarine* (1933) would eventually try to capture the experience.

As a Liverpool adolescent I grew up in a house in Marine Terrace, Waterloo which gave a fine view from my bedroom window of the ships coming and going on the Mersey. In the 1960s, the port was still busy with the Canadian Pacific and Cunard liners that came out with booming sirens on the Friday night tide as we trained our binoculars on them, their comings and goings traceable in the *Journal of Commerce*. The traffic, from what the novelist John Brophy called this 'city of departures', always seemed to speak to me of escape and of the thrilling passage to elsewhere. But I stayed put, and it would be another twenty years before I finally broke out.

In our mid-thirties my wife and I quit our jobs, sold our house, and set off on a long trip around the world with not the slightest heed to what would happen when we came back. We flew to Hong Kong and travelled through China, Thailand, Malaysia, Singapore, Indonesia, Australia, New Zealand and the United States. Four nights was the longest we spent in any one place during those eight and a half months. There was a lot of stasis, a lot of ennui, to burn out of our system. Fetching up in the antipodean winter of 1988 at Dunedin, with no reading matter left, I fished out of a junk-shop box a hardback copy of the first American edition of Lowry's *October Ferry to Gabriola*. It was one of those books that hit you with a shock of recognition, seeming destined for you personally at the very time you pick them up, addressing themselves as if by design to your condition.

I still have that same 1970 rust-coloured World Publishing Company edition in front of me as I write.

It was a book about a man and wife who turned their back on conventional life in early middle age and, in a sense, 'dropped out' – once again, before dropping out had been invented. And the man was from Liverpool, the registered port of the wreck *Eridanus* that lay beneath the water in the Vancouver inlet where Lowry's squatter's shack rose from wooden piles on the beach: 'And on the stern, seeming to comment on my own source, for I too had been born in the terrible city whose main street is the ocean, could still be almost made out the ghost of the words: *Eridanus*, Liverpool.'[1] Clearly this was a book I was destined to read.

---

1   'The Forest Path to the Spring', in *Hear Us O Lord from Heaven Thy Dwelling Place* (Harmondsworth: Penguin Modern Classics, 1979 [1961]), p. 226.

From the more rigorous critical standpoint such an approach to a book might seem at best frivolous, at worst downright inadmissible, but Lowry's fiction was written in the era of the post-war *nouveau roman* just then being invented by novelists such as Alain Robbe-Grillet – in which, if the full-blooded postmodernist permission to possess the text and make of it whatever we as readers want had not yet been granted, a certain modernist undecidability, an openness to multiple interpretation, the reader as much as the author contributing to the process, seemed appropriate and in the spirit of Lowry's writing.

October Ferry is a complex book that grew from a simple short story originally written in collaboration with his wife Margerie (who came, 'by a commodious vicus of recirculation' – to borrow a phrase from James Joyce, an author much admired by Lowry – to edit the final text for posthumous publication in 1970) to become a multi-layered work that cost its author much pain. But two primary themes, for me, stand out. The first: the shared pursuit, by a couple in love, of an ideal existence, their search for an embodiment, a local habitation, for that ideal. An actual dwelling place, if not of bricks and mortar, then of weather-silvered cedar timbers and sunken piles. The second: the knowledge that we are fated, at some point, to be evicted from Eden and had therefore better not get too attached to it. Lowry understood the meaning of Paradise: that it is desired and that it is nowhere. Huxley and Orwell taught the mid-twentieth century that Utopia can be toxic. Lowry absorbed, but was not defeated by, that lesson, in a book alert to the moment of its making: Cold War state paranoia, environmental degradation, cultural trivialisation, all coming to focus 'at the end of this fourth year of the atomic age'.[2]

But first the pain. The agony is set out in Lowry's published letters. *October Ferry* was first announced in September 1947, almost a year after the journey that Malcolm and Margerie took in search of a replacement for their squatter's shack on the beach at Dollarton, British Columbia which was threatened with demolition by the authorities, who wanted to bulldoze these illegal settlements to make way for a civic park. But it was not until 1950 that the draft, with the working title *Eridanus*, was resumed, with Lowry taking back full charge of what was still a novella. He told his agent, Harold Matson, on 2 October 1951 that it was now 'completely redrafted and largely rewritten, and it deals with the theme of eviction, which is related to man's dispossession, but this theme is universalised. This I believe to be a hell of a fine thing.'[3] The letter captures perfectly the tone of edgy, if not abject, assertiveness writers are forced to adopt when writing to their agents and publishers, but the story was to continue to cause Lowry trouble, and one can follow its long, troubled gestation in the pages of the collected letters throughout 1952 and 1953 as the 'novella' grew into a full-length novel.

In April 1953, Margerie wrote to Lowry's publisher, Albert Erskine: 'Malc is engaged in a life & death struggle with this bloody story, which seems to have turned into a

---

2 *October Ferry to Gabriola*, first US edition (New York: World Publishing Company, 1970), p. 227.
3 *Sursum Corda! The Collected Letters of Malcolm Lowry. Volume II: 1947 – 1957*, ed. Sherrill E. Grace (London: Jonathan Cape, 1996), p. 436.

novel, & he's determined to get through to the end this week before it kills us both [...] October Ferry to Gabriola is going to be first rate Lowry. At the moment it is, to me, a vampire, a tiger, a merciless tyrant but I *think* we are going to survive & defeat the goddam thing after all.'[4] In June, Lowry told Erskine that 'this damned thing' has 'cost me more pains than all the Volcano put together [...] What crisis was the author passing through [...] The answer to this question I can only say must be found in Gabriola itself, which I more & more see – though perhaps half-humorously – almost as a challenge to the author's actual personal salvation.'[5]

In his longest letter about the novel, putting himself into the third person, Lowry wrote: 'And in Gabriola he has turned what set out to be an innocent & beautiful story of human longing into quite one of the most guilt-laden & in places quite Satanically horrendous documents it has ever been my unfortunate lot to read, let alone have to imagine I wrote. One saving grace is that it is in places incredibly funny, I think.' The letter, which finally peters out in mid-sentence, and wasn't actually sent, is not wholly coherent, but it asserts that the novel is

> a psychological triumph of the first order [...] here the challenge seemed – and seems – ultimate, a matter of life or death, – & rebirth – as it were, for its author, not to say sanity or otherwise: perhaps I overstate the case, but my love for this place & my fear of losing it, nay actual terror, had begun to exceed all bounds; moreover the tactile objective threat has been horrible for me beyond words – which is part of the point, alas: not Dante's personal spiritual position when he wrote the Inferno was worse, & I shall have no Inferno to show for it, only, with luck a piece of prose which if it manages to live at all – and it just might – will no doubt do so for the wrong reason, & for a reason which might well condemn it as a work of art... namely that the bloody agony of the writer writing it is so patently extreme that it creates a kind of power in itself, that together with the humour & what lyricism it may possess, takes your mind off the faults of the story itself, which, incidentally, are of every kind – in fact it possessed perhaps not one single conventional virtue of the normal story, – its character drawing is virtually non-existent, symbols are pointed at blatantly instead of being concealed or subsumed in the material or better, simply real & not there at all, it is – or is as it stands – repetitious to the point beyond that which you can believe it's all done on purpose, & some readers – if they read it once – might have to read it 5 times before they could be convinced anything has happened at all [...] And it does have some aesthetic virtues. It starts gently, so gently... [6]

This extraordinary outburst of candour and artistic self-awareness hits some legitimate targets and shows that Lowry was aware that *October Ferry* was not a perfect creation; but what we have is still, I believe, a remarkable achievement. What, then, was the source of this torment?

---

4   *Letters*, p. 641.
5   *Letters*, p. 659.
6   *Letters*, p. 664.

October Ferry to Gabriola takes place, like Joyce's *Ulysses*, over one single day, 7 October 1949, the twentieth anniversary of the suicide of the friend of its central character, Ethan Llewellyn. Peter Cordwainer's undergraduate suicide was one that Ethan could have prevented and one that he may even have encouraged by hinting that he would follow Peter. It is also the hundredth anniversary of the death of Edgar Allan Poe, whose spirit inhabits some of the more macabre moments of the novel. Like a mad motif throughout the book, Ethan keeps seeing a roadside advertising hoarding that promotes 'Mother Gettle's kettle-simmered soup', a billboard that uses the image of the youthful Cordwainer, whose father was the advertising manager of the soup company. Ethan is a criminal barrister who has thrown in his job in order to seek, with his wife Jacqueline, a new home after the destruction of their earlier home at Niagara-at-the-Lake, and the threat of eviction from their next home, a beach-side shack near Vancouver. They take a Greyhound bus from Victoria on Vancouver Island to Nanaimo in the north of the island, where the ferry departs for Gabriola, one of the still unspoilt islands of the Gulf of Georgia, between Vancouver Island and the British Columbia mainland. This bald summary more or less contains the 'action' of the novel. In an afterword to the posthumous first publication, Margerie Lowry explained that the author never succeeded in finding a way of including the additional idea that Ethan might have quit his job when he discovered that the seemingly innocent man he had defended was in fact guilty of a horrendous murder.

Lowry, as well as endlessly reworking his fiction, and often keeping several projects simultaneously in active motion, also wove into everything he wrote versions of himself, and, more importantly, versions of his obsessions and fears. Even without the suicide as a metaphor of guilt, Lowry seems to have had enough psychic darkness to spare lurking in his own consciousness. There are indeed passages that articulate extreme fears and obsessive guilt, disordered mental states, reminiscent of *Under the Volcano*, but there is also that humour he identified in his letter. There is bright sunlight in this book as well as the storm clouds of threat and anxiety.

Two or three short stories preceded *October Ferry* in describing or, more accurately, hymning the felicities of the earthly paradise at Dollarton near to Vancouver where the Lowrys lived from 1940 to 1953. The short story 'The Forest Path to the Spring' is the happiest recreation of that period and can be read as a taster for *October Ferry*, but there are similarly attractive passages in the novel where that beach-side idyll is described, bringing forth some of Lowry's most lyrical prose. He wrote exquisitely and with extreme tenderness of the beauties of their inlet, the simplicity of their life together, the swimming from the wooden jetty at dawn and dusk, the flowers, the alighting gulls, the changes of light, the patterns made by sun and moon, the texture of rainfall. He also wrote of the pleasures of neighbourliness and the mutual aid offered by the fishermen and other shack-dwellers along the shore of the inlet. And at the heart of the book is the depiction of the relationship of Jacqueline and Ethan, frankly representing their quarrels and their tensions, but ultimately celebrating the life of two 'lucky strangers' who had rediscovered Arcadia:

Happy, they indeed had been, like spirits in some heaven of the Apocalypse or in some summerland of spiritualists, spirits who had no right to be where they were, which was their only source of doubt, when they doubted it.

But the reverse of their bliss was nothing like infelicity. It resembled terror, a great wind, or a recurrent suspicion of a great wind, the Chinook itself. What he felt dimly they repressed then was anguish on a greater scale than two human hearts were meant to contain, as though their own heart had been secretly drawing to itself some huge accumulating sorrow: alien sorrow, for which there was no longer scarcely the slightest shred of sympathy to be found in the so-called liberal thought of which they imagined themselves the enlightened partakers. Steam, trade, machinery had long banished from it all romance and seclusion. (pp. 66-67)

It was thus a realistic paradise, facing a vista of oil refineries, saw mills and logging camps, shipping, occasional oil-slicks, as well as mists and golden light and far vistas of mountain and forest. And there were the tabloid newspapers, periodically inveighing against the tax-dodging squatters, eyesores, bad citizens of the modern Canadian state. This was not Thoreau at the glittering purity of Walden Pond, this was post-war, McCarthyite north America, seen by Lowry the proto-Green with perfect clarity and an absence of self-delusion: 'What he really wanted was to be free of the whole false view of life, false comforts constrained by advertisements and monstrous deceptions, what more valuable gesture could they have made in this age?' (p. 154). Lowry, of course, was interested in the occult and the meaning of coincidence. Ethan reads in his cabin a copy of the cabbala and finds it helpful:

In fact he could sum up no better their life on the beach than to say it had been, in a manner, *his* cabbala, in the sense that, if he was not mistaken, that system might be regarded on one plane as a means less of accumulating than of divesting oneself – by arrangement, balancing them against opposites – of unbalanced ideas: the mind finally transcending both aspects, regains its lost equilibrium, or for the first time truly discovered it: not unlike, Ethan sometimes supposed, the modern process of psychoanalysis. (p. 169)

Ethan was seeking, as Malcolm and Margerie sought, a way of life that, in the contemporary world, held meaning. It was not the world of New World respectability and sobriety, of political quietism and obedience, of conventional life. It was opposed to the destruction of the world's natural resources, ascetic but realistic about its dependency on such modern inventions as the bus which takes them to Vancouver and its libraries. It was paralleled by Lowry's art of fiction, an exploratory, cumulative, inclusive art of balance and counterpoint, every component seen as relating to every other – he wanted his entire opus to be known by the collective rubric of *The Voyage that Never Ends*. The voyage never does end, the pilgrimage, the quest, rarely finds its grail and is recommenced. Ethan and Jacqueline finally arrive at Nanaimo at the end of the novel, and, after a last, nightmarish brush with the world of modern consumer capitalism in the shape of the hideously revamped Men's Bar of the Ocean Spray inn

121

near the ferry dock, they set sail. We do not know if they will find another Eridanus on the island of Gabriola; if they will find themselves, in their own private jargon, once again 'in the current'.

'Could it be,' Ethan speculates in the closing pages,

> that it was rather as if, on our journey through life, some guardian spirit causes our attention to be drawn, at such moments, to certain combinations, whether of events, or persons, or things, but which we recognize, as speaking to us in a secret language, to remind us that we are not altogether unwatched, and so encourage us to our highest endeavour, and especially is this true when we most need help, which is almost the same as saying when we most need assurance that our lives are not valueless? (p. 320)

October Ferry to Gabriola, as Lowry feared, is occasionally a flawed novel, but it is a richly rewarding and haunting one in its celebration of human freedom and the determination to find a meaningful path or embark on the redeeming voyage. Of course it can be criticised for such things as its lack of action, its under-developed characters (such as Jacqueline's father 'The McCandless', the shaman, of whom we could happily have seen a lot more), the strained passages of 'coincidence' when houses burn with too insistent a symbolism, the curious unconvincingness of the dialogue at certain points, the sometimes shakily extended, grammatically precarious, long sentences. But in the end this is a story of the aspiration towards a better life that is not necessarily 'escapist' and it resonates with me still, twenty years after my own adventure. My own refusal.

Cian Quayle, film still, 2009

Courtesy of the Artist

UXORIOUS PROSE: MALCOLM LOWRY'S OCTOBER FERRY TO GABRIOLA

Poster for the Malcolm Lowry Room

Michael Turner Fonds, W.A.C. Bennett Library, Special Collections and Rare Books Division,
Simon Fraser University, Vancouver

The Malcolm Lowry Room

Michael Turner

The Malcolm Lowry Room was a 99-seat nightclub in the North Burnaby Inn, located at 4125 East Hastings Street, six blocks east of the municipality of Vancouver and within mortar fire of Lowry's wartime Dollarton home. I opened the club in August 1993, after seven years in a 'postmodern jugband', touring some of the cruellest clubs on the planet. Of course the last thing I wanted, upon retirement, was to get into the bar business. But that's exactly what happened. Not long after my final tour I was asked by my brother-in-law, the NBI's manager, if I might help him revive the hotel's lounge, draw on my music connections and book some bands.

The lounge was an amputated version of a 300-seat biker bar known as the Sting Cabaret. This was back in the day when the NBI was called the Admiral, its façade shaped to look like the steamships that travelled up and down the British Columbia coast. Before the lounge had been conceived, the Sting stretched the length of the hotel's west side to include an area that would later be sealed off and used alternately for keg storage and mysterious invite-only 'special events'. The total area accounted for almost half the NBI's ground floor, while on the east side, its equal – a 300-seat strip bar known as the Pub, where exotic dancers slithered down poles, took off their clothes, and showered. Separating the Pub and the lounge was a lobby and an eight-table café. Upstairs, a horseshoe of twenty-four rooms – some occupied by long-term residents, others by the hour.

How the Sting became a lounge is a story unto itself. The quick version goes like this: in order for the NBI to open an off-sales beer and wine store, the City of Burnaby, under pressure from a Sting-intolerant Royal Canadian Mounted Police, intimated that a licensing application might go easier if the Sting were to close. A deal was struck, whereby in exchange for an off-sales licence the Sting would shrink by seventy per cent, with the remaining thirty per cent becoming a lounge.

The Characters Lounge was a hopelessly unintelligent affair, an oak and brass disaster where dead ferns hung from the ceiling and the walls were covered in brewery promo. My first visit there took place on a hot July afternoon, mid-week. I entered from the lobby, just as the bartender was chasing down someone for walking out with a piece of brass railing. Just as well, I thought – the joint looks better without it. Indeed, calling this lounge Characters spoke more to its three sullen regulars than to anything a place that dead might inspire. Converting Characters from a generic sports bar into an out-of-the-way alternative nightclub would be difficult. Because I like a challenge, I said yes. But it was a conditional yes. If I were to do this, it would have to be on my terms. Beginning with the name.

Vancouver, like many west coast cities, has never been good at history – the smart money being on the future, not the past. First the gold rush, then the Vancouver Stock Exchange, and more recently, real estate speculation. Only lately has the city become

Poster for the Malcolm Lowry Room
Michael Turner Fonds, W.A.C. Bennett Library, Special Collections and Rare Books Division,
Simon Fraser University, Vancouver

THE MALCOLM LOWRY ROOM
4125 East Hastings St.

October 1 & 2

A solo / acoustic evening with

ART
BERGMANN
plus special guests

with a 9:00 screening of
Bruce MacDonald's
Highway 61
(featuring Art Bergmann, thespian)

• NO COVER •
• Presented by CJSF •

Sometimes you want to go where nobody knows your name...
For more information, please contact Michael Turner at 685-5317

Poster for the Malcolm Lowry Room
Michael Turner Fonds, W.A.C. Bennett Library, Special Collections and Rare Books Division,
Simon Fraser University, Vancouver

interested in its history. But in August 1993, history was revolutionary. Which is how I came up with the Malcolm Lowry Room.

Lowry lived here. He was a writer, musician, film buff and drinker, and these were the things I wanted to encourage. Alternative bands at the weekends, jazz on Thursdays, an open microphone on Wednesdays, and an unofficial film night on Tuesdays – all of which could be experienced under the influence of cheap pints and free admission. But first things first – I needed to renovate.

My first stop was the University of British Columbia's Special Collections Library, where I selected five Lowry photographs, to be enlarged, printed and framed. Lowry holding his beloved Bols in front of his Dollarton shack would go above the fake fireplace. An earlier photo of him in a suit playing his taropatch would go beside the stage. Near the entrance, Lowry in his bathing trunks, standing guard. At the same time I trolled local junk stores looking for paintings reminiscent of the Lowry oeuvre. A tramp steamer, like the one in *Ultramarine*. A BC ferry, like the one in *October Ferry to Gabriola*. A half-completed paint-by-numbers of the Panama Canal, after my favourite Lowry text, the collagist 'Through the Panama'. I also copied and enlarged one of Lowry's poems, 'Christ Walks in This Infernal District Too', whose opening lines – 'Beneath the Malebolge lies Hastings Street/ The province of the pimp upon his beat/ For each in his little world of drugs and crime/ Moves helplessly or, hopeful, begs a dime' – seemed appropriate, even though the club was at the wrong end of Hastings. What I could not find I had commissioned: volcano sculptures, paintings of forest walks, a Day of the Dead festival, a portrait of Margerie in bed with Albert Finney. As for the stage, I repurposed a trapezoid valance that hid a bank of cheap disco lights aimed at an eight-by-ten-foot dance floor, attaching two pieces of crushed red velvet at either side, the drapes tied near the bottom by gold braided ropes. Beside the drapes, two PA speakers. All that was left were the bookings.

Like Lowry, the NBI is well-known to Vancouverites – but it is a surface knowledge. Most scholars recognise Lowry as our city's first Modern novelist, though many regard him as an unreadable drunk. The NBI, on the other hand, was home to the annual Christmas party of the Vancouver chapter of the world's wealthiest motorcycle club – but is in fact a complex social organism, a kind of cooperative feudal manor brokered by Sicilian *padrone*, with a dash of dynastic Chinese blood feud mixed in. My goal was to open Lowry's work to the public, but in an unstable environment – fear being a good way to heighten one's senses.

Because of the neighbouring strip bar, I decided to open with an all-girl band. cub were a local trio who wrote catchy tunes and acerbic lyrics, and drew crowds. And the media loved it, picking up on the irony that had ball-busting women performing on one side of the hotel, compliant wood nymphs on the other – not to mention the lie I told them about how Lowry, desperate for a drink, swam the half-mile width of Burrard Inlet, climbed the bluff, and walked the remaining eight blocks to the Admiral (which, now that I think about it, might not have been built yet). Although licensed for ninety-nine, over two hundred people showed up, three of them visiting record executives who mistook the MLR for the Pub, after which one of them told me how they waited an hour before assuming the show was cancelled, all the while wondering how cub would get their drum kit down that pole.

One thing I was not told – something that caused me a great deal of stress in the four years the club was open – was that due to licensing regulations, the Pub stopped serving drinks at 1 pm, while the MLR remained open until two. During the first month this was not a problem; the MLR was over-the-top-popular, and crowds are their own buffer. It was only later, once things died down, that drunken Pub patrons would arrive en masse, only to find themselves shushed by a circle of twenty-something men in cardigans, one of whom was playing Carpenters covers on a toy piano. These were gut-wrenching confrontations, and after every one of them I was convinced my audience would move on. But no, word got out of someone's bravery (usually their restraint, as opposed to a punch thrown), and the curious kept coming.

Something I learned during my time at the MLR concerned the Pub clientele – those I feared most were not the bikers but the likes of the cocaine-addled 33-year-old twice-divorced roofer living in his parents' basement. Generally speaking, this was the most unpredictable of men, an intolerant frightened individual with muscles just big enough to pick on those smaller, of either sex. These were the patrons most intimidated by my alternative programme, not the bikers. Indeed, one of our finest nights ever was when a Detroit-based punk band called the Demolition Doll Rods rolled into town. This was a band that performed naked but for carefully placed pieces of gaffer tape, with two of the members in the midst of gender reassignment. The bikers, being self-professed freaks, cheered them on. But not the roofer. Too threatened. If Lowry had been there, I wonder who among the Pub clientele he would have chosen to sit with. One thing's for sure, in the four years the MLR was in operation, the kids on my side loved him.

Ray Lowry, *Untitled (Under the Volcano series)*, 2008,
acrylic on paper, 30 x 42 cm

Courtesy of See Gallery

Ray Lowry, *Untitled (Under the Volcano series)*, 2008,
mixed media, mainly ink, on paper, 42 x 30 cm

Jorge Martínez García, *El Abismo*: *La Barranca*, 2007, drypoint, lavis (wash)
and roulette on aluminium, BFK rives paper, 24.7 x 33.7 cm, edition of 22

Courtesy of the Artist and Craig Scott Gallery, Toronto

Malcolm Lowry's land

Robert Sheppard

The sensation produced by reading these notes was really rather curious.[1]

Malcolm Lowry

You set off, at break of mid-morning, hung-over, mouth acidic with vomit from the night before. You carry an empty notebook groggily into brilliant sunlight, for – as Lowry puts it – **the peculiar stichometry of his observations, jotted down as if he were writing a species of poem.**[2] The text measures your walk, 'Catch Points: Southwick-Lewes-Ripe'. Your Zenit camera, with its logo for the coming Moscow Olympics, rests in your bag. It is 4th March 1979.

'The sleepy dormitory town,' you write, and take its picture. *From the railway station platform part of Southwick is visible: the Victorian villas tightly shunted together opposite The Green. A war memorial brushed into one corner records the names of members of families I went to school with: Upperton, Penfold. Only one or two isolated cars putter up the road skirting it* where nowadays there is constant traffic. *Above the level rooftops, the spire of St Michael's, rebuilt after the Second World War, pierces a frosty blue sky, small puffy clouds set at irregular distances, like an academic painting. Further off, the* **Great South Downs**, *as Margerie Bonner Lowry called them, sloping, sandy-hewed in the early spring light, beneath them a dark ridge of trees where West Sussex Downland folds onto the houses.* Today, edge-land retail palaces impose their imperial roof styles across this townscape.

Your psychosomatic theory of thought – which at least rejects Cartesian dualism in favour of impassioned intellection, out of Nietzsche – guides your every remark, screens out the contagions of contingency. This week, you believe in the pop determinism of 'Biorhythms', and today is your Sensitivity Critical Day. On such a day, Japanese pilots would become so worried that they might plough their aircraft into mountains and volcanoes, they'd excuse themselves from flying. You shouldn't have been let out of bed. Worse than this, it is Sunday.

You don't remember the black girl in dungarees at Lewes station, don't remember how you discovered that there were no buses to Ripe on Sundays. Unlike Lowry, you approach the 'Authorities', you note. The policemen give you two routes, recommend the quicker but add that they'd probably have to send out a search party to find you at midnight. They laugh. I wonder whether either of them was veteran enough to have

---

1   Malcolm Lowry, 'Strange Comfort Afforded by the Profession', in *Hear Us O Lord from Heaven Thy Dwelling Place* (Harmondsworth: Penguin Books, 1969), p. 107.

2   Lowry, 'Strange Comfort', p. 104.

been on duty around here on 27th June 1957. It's only twenty-two years before. **One evening last week Mrs. Marjorie Lowry, of White Cottage, Ripe, tried to stop her 47-year-old writer-husband, Clarence, from starting on the gin. She smashed the bottle on the floor. And he hit her. Afraid, Mrs. Lowry fled next door, and did not go back to the cottage until nine o'clock the next morning. When she did she found her husband dead. This was the story told at the Eastbourne inquest.** *Evening Argus,* **2nd July 1957.**[3] Each of these statements has been doubted since, especially by the police. These officers wave you off. You take the longer, surer, A-road route, which allows you to rest at the Trevor Arms at Glynde for a shandy. Remember, you've a hangover. You're told you're barmy by the barman for trying to walk, though it's only five miles. You report none of this in the final poem. You pass a pub called The Manxman and devise a terrible pun about Manx writers having no tales. Might Lowry – elective Manxman – have seen this pub sign during the few months he lived at Ripe? It might have brought a smile to his face. He might have even read it as a good omen. He needed one.

You note: 'the first Spring day,/ the soft sloped hills,/ the alluvial valley,/ the country silence,' an attempted objectivism at least, as you trudge on. There would have been less traffic on these main roads then, room to savour that 'country' silence that is not silence, always disturbed by distant humans, engines humming languidly or coughing. **Drivers of LARGE or SLOW Vehicles must phone to get permission to cross** the railway line, or maybe it was a bridge over the river. You merely record the legend. Your 'bitterness in the face of enthusiasm' – you keep quoting Flaubert to yourself – is trumped up by the supposed emotions of your sensitivity crisis.[4] What things must escape your eye, your pen! But this sign-writer is more precise, comically so, and you plagiarise: **LARGE means over 55 feet long or 9 feet 6 inches wide or 32 tons total weight.** You stop to take another photograph. *Wedged into the ploughed earth, speckled with stubble, scattered with rootless straws, the can's label is clearly legible:* **CYDRAX,** as if dropped there as a symbol. A non-alcoholic cider – which Lowry tried to drink after coming out of Atkinson Morley Hospital, on his return to Ripe. Among the debris that you note, but don't photograph, there are 'fuck-books', fleshy shreds of desire torn and tossed about by some rural masturbator. Lowry was accused of being an onanist by a surviving friend, as if that meant anything – more pop psychology! Later, you visit a shop in a petrol station, for what you don't say. A transistor radio crackles out Thin Lizzy.

'Crows croak,' you write, suddenly alive to things, 'as I disturb them/ taking wing from brittle nests in wirework trees,' trunk by trunk, branch by branch, as you pass along the entwined row marking the edge of a field, black windbreak. This is a place of death for you too, you remember. Perhaps you hadn't realised that this walk would bring you so close to your own 'Open Verdict', 'Death by Misadventure', and

---

3   Quoted in Douglas Day, *Malcolm Lowry* (London: Oxford University Press, 1973), p. 4; and in Gordon Bowker, *Pursued by Furies: A Life of Malcolm Lowry* (New York: St Martin's Press, 1997), p. 602.

4   The original 1979 poem references 'Flaubert, repeatedly in his *Nile Journal*', from which I believe I heard extracts on a BBC radio programme.

the unignorable symbolism of the dreadful place-name. **Police today appealed for help in filling in details of the last five days in the life of 21-year-old John Charles Purdy. Mr Purdy, a laboratory technical assistant at Sussex University, and who lived at Southwick, was found dead on the Downs at Black Cap, near Plumpton, last Saturday.** *Evening Argus,* 15th January 1976. As with Lowry's death – and with that mysterious death within the youthful Lowry's life – there are only questions that last decades, and unlocatable guilt for his friends. The copy of *Astral Weeks* with his blood on the cover, the thing that is left to us.

The neat leafless hedge runs along the side of the road, edging the field, curves toward the distant church, which coyly crouches between, under, two enormous evergreens. One bears a vast, lurching canopy, the other sports branches in symmetrical saucer-shaped layers, floating, as though planted upside down. I'm intoxicated by your photograph. *But everything else is predictable in Ripe, a perfect North American dream of East Sussex, a suitable retreat for an alcoholic. A terrace with tall, Jacobean chimneys, a square squat cottage with black window-frames – like the Lowrys' White Cottage, but isn't.* **SLOW means 5 mph or less.** *Long shadows carpet the narrow lane down which a cyclist recedes like a figure in a dream.*

In the rawest notes, along with the 'heralding' cockerel and the 'funereal' church bells of Ripe that survive into the poem, you denote: 'the girl on the broken bridge above the stream'. She dallies there like a culpable spy in a Lowry fragment, set up to reappear like a coincidence. She's escaped until this moment, is resurrected even, 30 years late, intact, inviolate because she's untouched by any memory, its failures, its compensatory fictiveness. I read her for the first time.

The clock on the Church of St John the Baptist tells me it's 25 to four. I peep through winter trees barely knobbly with buds, fisted tight against the growing cold that I sense in the watery blue air dropping frosty towards earth. All life is harbouring underground. A brick tower, washed in the same sandy light as this morning, castellated at its tip, wide-buttressed below. Mean east windows, possibly stained, but probably just latticed with lead, darken the interior. Broken fences draped with brittle brambles, thornset. You approach carefully, step through to search, camera at the ready, lens cap in your pocket. You record the moment. 'The sudden shock of the grave: /**Malcolm Lowry 1909-1957.**' *This modest plot* is 'budding with daffodils its length' you write. Looking again, they might be crocuses, with their bitter chalices still clenched by winter. *A stubby slab, as though but half-risen from the earth, the name and date clearly chiselled. Tufty grass on this shifty, uneven, but untrodden ground. Sunken graves with tilted headstones surround it.* In a late version of the poem I find: 'no goldenrod in a gin bottle/ as homage!' It's somebody else's anecdote about visiting this place, something he or she found here. In any case, you wouldn't recognise goldenrod, even from Lowry's writing, which merely names it. Instead I think of the legendary bottle of Flower's bitter, emptied on the grave's first closing over, a piss-puddle on the fresh soil.

'The uncertain pilgrimage/ to the grave //strange comfort,' you remark, and then quote Lowry's story to describe yourself: **He put the notebook and pencil back in his** pocket, glanced around him again with a heavier, more penetrating look – that in fact was informed by such a malaise he saw nothing at all but which was intended to say 'I have a perfect right to do this,' or 'If you saw me do that, very well then, I *am* some sort of detective....'[5] 'The paranoid detective/ with camera & notebook/ retires,' returns to Southwick, you state, recording nothing of the walk and train journey back. You are away about eight hours. Except the thought that you – he – I – we are all 'walking back into the future'. This is certainly true in one way you cannot imagine, now I'm writing this account through yours, too belated to be revising your words. I'm trying to trail processes of subjectivation, not the products of your subjectivity.

You're 'too tired/ for the appropriate emotions' – or your body is, you scribble – at the chill graveside, and spare me your biorhythmic complexities, the ambivalent pieties of which might leave me reeling with laughter! You've got that hangover to play with. Yet even you concede the peril of 'self-immolation on the pyre of one's own emotions' (though I remove one of your adjectives). This could be a hard reflection upon Lowry's failure of method, or of your own. You never publish the poem. Lowry's continual cycles of drinking connect to his failure of focus. Fecund and feculent both. Too often no other subject than his own self and its neurotic involutions, erotic insulations, would suffice. His love of booze, his fear of the pox. Except for during those lucid moments hours days months, when the world flooded him, when he noticed how Pompeii reminded him of **the ruins of Liverpool on a Sunday afternoon** or whatever, and he assembled his notebook jottings and versions into fiction in all its clinker-built brilliance.[6] I must resist the taropatch-twirling legend with a near-empty gin bottle protruding from his grimy trenchcoat pocket, grinning like a red rubber monkey in tricky-cheeriness, squinting through his feline eyes, and lurching into this homage just before closing time. I am a life-long member of the covenanted Lowry fraternity, true. People either 'get' Lowry or they don't. It's a matter of recognition, attunement to an existential rhythm that runs through the writing (not a biorhythm in sight), a wavering oscillation carrying bitterness and enthusiasm. They are books in which something thought is thought to be enacted, but isn't, and yet at some other level, it is, like an unspoken declaration of love for the world. Books unforgettably totemic, quite unreliable and dangerous to know. They threaten to erupt and flow from their central fumarole of genius. But I must resist seeing this clowning as a deranged release from convention or as a sign of that 'genius', as too many did, until hurt. I am attempting to erase all such fictions from this account, but know I continue to see my own selves there too, much as Lowry did, assuming his various guises, however doubtfully.

In the last, rough note of the day, you prepare yourself for later revision. 'Tired. Read again after dinner. ONLY ESSENTIALS.' **Yet how he hated to write it down (loved to see it in print?)**, you quote, **though like so much with him it had little reality unless he did.**[7] 'ONLY ESSENTIALS,' you re-read, sinking into the bed in the darkening room,

---

5   Lowry, 'Strange Comfort', p. 99. This quotation forms part of the original 1979 poem.
6   Malcolm Lowry, 'Present Estate of Pompeii', in *Hear Us O Lord*, p. 183.
7   Lowry, 'Strange Comfort', p. 102. This quotation forms part of the original 1979 poem.

re-living the day as you select, slimming it down. The black girl at Lewes, the jocular policemen, the incredulous barman, the suspect girl on the bridge, and their things, are all delivered from the poem. Until I recover them from notebooks and versions, celebrate that they exist, again. Writing is always somewhere else.

*   *   *

Wednesday, 4th March 2009

It's 30 years to the day. A sunny morning, trying to hold onto its threat of rain. Over the high wall at the end of the Southwick eastbound platform, the old view is blocked by abrupt abutments: roofs of Georgian-style dwellings, covered by patches of moss the colour of ear-wax. The London launch of *Warrant Error* brings me back for this anniversary, a suspicious coincidence. I thought to repeat my journey to Ripe, a symmetry all-too-neat, with some trepidation, recalling the disaster of Lowry's return to Mexico. I resist willing experience.

Practicalities killed it off, in any case. Over the web I tracked my virtual route, discovered only one bus to Ripe per fortnight, a Thursday, unthinkable in Lowry's day, and even in the 1970s. I'm uncertain whether I should test my weakened ankle on the thick band the on-line route-planner sweeps across the landscape, a smooth blue carpet without bump, ruck or trough, labelled 'walking'. More than this, in the viral space of the internet, I catch the easy images that replace discovery, recovery. His grave once more, defaced now by something like the moss that clings to the roofs, near-unreadable. Margerie's tombstone – not there in 1979, of course – taller, almost pedantic by comparison, with its details, separate like a withheld verdict. White Cottage – I suddenly remember I failed to find it 30 years ago – with a blue plaque announcing Lowry's domicile, but not his death there: a bad detail for real estate exchange in today's catastrophic market.

Customers for Lewes should change at Brighton. I scramble out at Hove then, head back as quickly as I can towards Lowry's place of birth, not death. Where I now live. It seems right. To this damaged landscape of stalled redevelopment, cranes frozen mid-clutch over abandoned concrete foundations. It has long erased the topology of Lowry's city of dreadful night: grim but febrile docks, pubs fragrant with scouse and Caegwyrle Ale, flickering flea-pits and sweaty Hippodromes. The Empire still stands, where Lowry saw Paul Whiteman, though he was then well past his orchestra's zenith, when Bix and Trumbauer had ridden high.

The clouds are woolly today, but dark and heavy along their flattened keels, sailing the bald slopes of the Downs, glimpsed once on the train's escape to London. Clustered like images of space itself, the eggshell blue of the sky beyond suggesting depth, infinitute. But what I search for is an image of time, until I realise that it's here already, in these sentences: the human elsewhen that enfolds the present, multiple genealogies of belatedness.

Jorge Martínez García, *Bajo el Volcan*, 2006, etching and soft ground on copper,
canson gravure paper, 50 x 70 cm, edition of 22

Courtesy of the Artist and Craig Scott Gallery, Toronto

138

Jorge Martínez García, *Rueda. Ley. Maquina. Sistema*, 2006, etching on bronze,
super alfa paper, 60 x 60 cm, edition of 44

Courtesy of the Artist and Craig Scott Gallery, Toronto

Jorge Martínez García, *Espiritus Del Mezcal*, 2006, etching and intaglio on zinc, super alfa paper, 23 x 25 cm, edition of 22

Courtesy of the Artist and Craig Scott Gallery, Toronto

Jorge Martínez García, *Tríptico: El Mezcal*, 2007, etching and softground on copper, arches cover paper, 40 x 25 cm; *El Volcan*, 2007, etching and softground on copper, arches cover paper, 40 x 40 cm; *Los Comisarios*, 2007, etching and softground on copper, arches cover paper, 40 x 25 cm. Each an edition of 22

Courtesy of the Artist and Craig Scott Gallery, Toronto

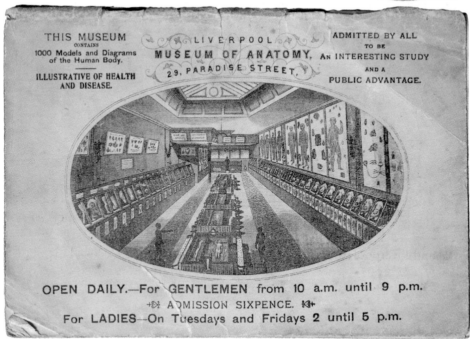

Descriptive catalogue of the Liverpool Museum of Anatomy in Paradise Street

Collection of Colin Dilnot

Malcolm Lowry: neglected genius

Gordon Bowker

Malcolm Lowry was once hailed as a successor to James Joyce and in 1947 his great novel *Under the Volcano* topped the *New York Times* bestseller list. But when he died ten years later in the sleepy Sussex village of Ripe, a month short of his forty-eighth birthday, none of his work was in print in his own language and his death passed more or less unnoticed. When the *Volcano* first appeared in England it was barely acknowledged. Most critics thought Lowry a Canadian or American, and in the austere late 1940s the literary climate favoured social realism. Only in the 1960s, when it was republished with most of his other novels, stories and letters, did British reviewers and scholars recognise Lowry's brilliance and claim him for English Literature.

He was born in New Brighton on 28 July 1909, 'within sight and sound of the sea and ships'.[1] Shortly after his birth, his family moved to Inglewood, a large mock-Tudor villa overlooking the Dee at Caldy. Arthur Lowry, his father, a cotton broker, commuted daily on the Mersey ferry from the Wirral to Liverpool – 'that terrible city whose main street is the ocean', Lowry wrote.[2] His mother, Evelyn, who, like Arthur, came from inner-city Toxteth, felt ill at ease in the upper-middle-class community to which she had been transplanted, and discouraged visitors to Inglewood. Malcolm was the youngest of four sons and an oddity – short, stocky, awkward, and mischievous. He feared his pious father ('a Tory of Tory capitalists on a grand scale'), hated his cold unfeeling mother ('a Methodist most wonderfully Methodistic'), and from his youth was determined to break free. He was proud of his maternal grandfather, an old sea-dog 'recalled by Old Hands in Liverpool' for his pugnacity and seamanship, but in *Ultramarine* he dismissed his parents with savage irony as demented syphilitics.

As a child the sea and ships enchanted him, and he saw the ocean as a means of escape. During the Great War his eldest brother, on leave from France, found him parading in front of the great bay window at Inglewood muttering, 'I wish I had a hook instead of a hand.' He read avidly and soon graduated from J. M. Barrie to Kipling and Rider Haggard's tales of derring-do.

The Wirral and Liverpool offered him a vision of heaven and hell. He loved the countryside around Caldy, but he was also fascinated by his 'City of Dreadful Night' – Liverpool – the bars, the docks and the questionable attractions of Paradise Street, where a horrifying museum warned unwary sailors against sinful encounters with ladies of the night. This place held a strange attraction for him, and he visited

---

1   For a fuller picture of Lowry's life, see my biography *Pursued By Furies: A Life of Malcolm Lowry*, originally published by HarperCollins in 1993 and now available from Faber as a 'Faber Finds' print-on-demand publication (see www.faber.co.uk/faberfinds).

2   Malcolm Lowry, 'The Forest Path to the Spring', in *Hear Us O Lord from Heaven Thy Dwelling Place & Lunar Caustic* (London: Picador, 1991), p. 226.

it frequently, even copying the directions and words of warning accompanying the disfigured foetuses, waxen effigies of ulcerated penises and 'the famous pickled testicles'. 'Man, Know Thyself' read the stern warning sign over the door. It was a vision of hell-fire no preacher could rival and it haunted him:

> I thought of [...] the faces of the poor people in Paradise Street, the waxworks, one little bit of light would have illuminated even the worst mass of corruption. This seemed [...] an exact picture of people's souls [...] I was fascinated by it & was going to go there again & again, I thought, I wouldn't be able to keep away from it 'a slave of the Museum of Anatomy' – as B. had been a slave of the picture palace.[3]

Not surprisingly, he became a syphilophobe, and the Paradise Street museum recurs in his fiction as a manifestation of damnation.

He was sent to Caldicott, a Hertfordshire prep school, and later to The Leys, a Methodist public school in Cambridge. Because he was small, clever and ungainly he was bullied and, when angry, would colour up like a lobster – hence his schoolboy nickname, 'Lobs' Lowry. At The Leys, 'Lobs' discovered jazz, writing and alcohol. His jazz heroes were Frankie Trumbauer and Bix Beiderbecke, and reading Rabelais gave him the idea that alcohol was an inspiration to the creative artist. Encouraged as a writer by a master on whom James Hilton had modelled his 'Mr Chips', he wrote quirky stories and comic sports reports for the school magazine in the manner of P. G. Wodehouse, as well as jazzy songs for the ukulele. He was specially excited by sea novels and plays: Joseph Conrad's *Typhoon*, Herman Melville's *Moby-Dick* and Eugene O'Neill's *Anna Christie* were particular favourites. Literature, the pen and the bottle became his escape routes from the tedious conventions of school and home.

He was an awkward, rough-and-tumble schoolboy rugby player, but a fine swimmer, a decent golfer and a clever if lazy scholar. He had a photographic memory, could recite long passage from books that gripped him, and developed what he called 'hysterical identifications' with certain writers. Discovering that Melville, on visiting Nathaniel Hawthorne, then US Consul in Liverpool, had declared his intention to be annihilated, he too felt somehow damned. That sense of doom hangs over most of his fictional protagonists, invariably outcasts or men (often writers) at odds with the world.

From boyhood he and his brothers played golf, both at Caldy and at Hoylake, where the greens and bunkers provided him with some of the strangest symbolic imagery in the *Volcano*, with the Consul's obscure references to the Donga (a sunken pathway to the seashore at Caldy) and to the names of old golf balls (such as the Zodiac Zone).

---

3   From handwritten notes to the MS of Lowry's early story, 'Enter One in Sumptuous Armour'. 'B' probably refers to the Lowry brothers' nurse, Miss Bell, whom they called 'Bey'.

At seventeen, he sailed to China and back as a deck-boy aboard the Liverpool freighter *Pyrrhus*. Unfortunately for Lowry, the crew resented a public schoolboy being handed a job while good seamen stood workless at the dock gates, and he was unmercifully bullied and sexually humiliated. But the experience gave him the material for his first novel.

Back in Caldy he began an account of his voyage, but his conventional family found him much changed. He spent nights on the town, often getting himself arrested for fighting in dockside bars. But then he discovered the American poet Conrad Aiken, whose novel *Blue Voyage* transfixed him and convinced him to become a novelist himself. He persuaded his father to let him go to Cambridge, Massachusetts to study under Aiken, provided he try for Cambridge entrance. The American was impressed by this handsome young Englishman, 'alight with genius', who knew his work better than he did, and the two entered into a strange, mutually destructive relationship. Aiken was a cynical, hard-bitten, hard-drinking, somewhat unstable character who set out to transform Lowry into a manipulable extension of himself, while Lowry was determined to take over Aiken's creative persona and outdo him. Unfortunately, while internalising Aiken's literary tastes and mindset he also internalised something of his mental volatility. His straightforward account of his China voyage now took on a strongly Aikenesque flavour, adopting the stream-of-consciousness method the American had taken from Joyce. He even borrowed fragments from *Blue Voyage*, which also suggested his title, *Ultramarine*. In this Aiken indulged him, but his readiness to borrow from others caused problems later. On the voyage home he read *The Ships Sails On* by the Norwegian Nordahl Grieg, a novel which inspired him as much as *Blue Voyage*. If the reactionary Aiken, his Dark Angel, had supplied him with a method of writing, the socialist Grieg, his Good Angel, gave him his plot – the dark voyage of the soul towards self-awareness.

In 1929, he entered St Catharine's College, Cambridge, where he soon established himself as a rather shady 'character'. During his first term, a friend, Paul Fitte, gassed himself aided by a drunken Lowry, and he was lucky to escape prosecution. Fitte became Wensleydale in *Dark as the Grave Wherein My Friend is Laid*, and thereafter a sense of guilt possessed Lowry, pervading much of his fiction. He was, said Aiken, 'a small boy chased by Furies'.

However, he soon acquired the more benign image of the drunken, ukulele-playing sailor-poet, crawling round the Cambridge pubs and turning out verse and inspired fiction for student magazines. The stories were extracts from *Ultramarine* – his *Portrait of the Artist as a Young Man* – which traces in highly poetic language the cruel initiation into manhood of his doppelganger, Dana Hilliot, aboard a China-bound Liverpool freighter. In it he reveals the ambivalence he felt towards Liverpool. Hilliot says that he comes from Liverpool, or thereabouts, and wants to imitate and adopt the language of his largely Liverpudlian shipmates. And yet he also claims to have been born in Norway and calls himself a 'Liverpool-Norwegian'. But a sense of Liverpool haunts the book and through it run images of the city – the Liver Building, Paradise

Street, and 'the viscous Mersey', 'like a vast camera film, slowly and inexorably winding'.[4]

After three years of dodging classes, he managed to scrape a degree by submitting an extract of *Ultramarine* to the examiners. With his novel finished he moved to London, pub-crawling around Fitzrovia drinking away the monthly stipend his father allowed him. *Ultramarine* was submitted to a London publisher, but when his manuscript was stolen from an editor's car Lowry contemplated suicide. Then fortunately he discovered that the friend who had typed the manuscript had preserved the carbon copy. The day was saved, and the book was published in 1933 by Jonathan Cape.

Although it got brief reviews in the *Times Literary Supplement* and the *New Statesman*, and the *Liverpool Daily Post* said that Lowry was the first harvest of the seeds of Lawrence and Joyce, *Ultramarine* was largely ignored. His mother, he liked to say, scandalised by its language, locked the book away.

On holiday in Spain, he met a vivacious young American, Jan Gabrial, fell passionately in love and in January 1934 married her secretly in Paris. Jan found him strange, a believer in mysticism and the occult. He prayed to strange gods and considered himself memeber of a ghostly family of dead authors, telling a friend that he frequently spoke to Kafka – which he probably did, drunk or sober.

The poor reception of his novel made Lowry feel rejected in England, and when Jan returned to America to inform her mother about her marriage, he followed her. For the next two and half years they lived in New York, where Malcolm began a long sea novel, *In Ballast to the White Sea* (based on a visit he had made to Nordahl Grieg in Oslo), in which the hero's father is a wealthy Liverpool shipping magnate.

Offering *Ultramarine* to an American publisher, Lowry was accused of plagiarism and threatened with exposure. Terrified, he sought the oblivion of alcohol, ending up in a Bellevue Hospital psychiatric ward where he remained for two weeks till Jan found him and had him discharged. But he had taken notes, and from that experience came *Lunar Caustic*, a brilliant surrealistic novella about the lunatic city, which fuses jazz and poetry and the ghost of Melville with the ramblings of demented sailors. However, fearing the charge of plagiarism, he became nervous of publishing, and only a French version of it appeared during his lifetime.

At the end of 1936 the Lowrys moved to Mexico, where Malcolm discovered the fiery liquor *mescal*, which had a devastating effect on him. He was fascinated by Mexico's strange death-cult, haunted the cantinas, got into fights and ended in jail. Then, on a bus journey to Cuautla, he and Jan saw an Indian who had been attacked and left to die at the roadside. This gave him the idea for a short story about a drunken British Consul who is casually murdered in Mexico. It was the germ of *Under the Volcano*.

Jan, despairing of his drinking, which intensified when Conrad Aiken visited them, left for Los Angeles. And so, his alcoholic Consul became a man deserted.

---

4   Malcolm Lowry, *Ultramarine* (Harmondsworth: Penguin, 1974 [1933]), pp. 131, 132.

Lowry once again descended into drink, was harassed by police and thrown into jail – all experiences religiously incorporated into his ever-expanding novel.

Threatened with expulsion from Mexico, he joined Jan in Hollywood, but their relationship never recovered. He then met Margerie Bonner, an ex-film actress, whom he married in 1940, settling down in a squatter's shack at Dollarton on the shores of Burrard Inlet near Vancouver. This became his 'Eridanus', the paradise in which he regained his peace of mind, and – despite the occasional lapse – his sobriety. At Dollarton he enjoyed the outdoor life, completed *Under the Volcano*, and, after a disastrous return trip to Mexico, wrote a series of short stories and drafts for three further novels. He planned to include all these works into a grand overarching epic entitle *The Voyage That Never Ends*, the aim of which, he said, was 'to give chaos a meaning, delirium a form'.

But this overambitious plan was bedevilled by setbacks. Always accident-prone, in June 1944 his shack burned down and he lost a thousand pages of *In Ballast*, the novel he had rewritten several times since first arriving in North America. Then, after the *Volcano* was published in 1947, he wasted a year in Europe, much of the time being drunk and close to madness. Back at Dollarton, his publisher declined his short story collection, *Hear Us O Lord from Heaven Thy Dwelling Place*, which threw him further off course, and he then became endlessly absorbed in *October Ferry to Gabriola*, a disappointing novel which led his publisher to cancel his contract.

During this period his last emotional links to Liverpool were finally severed. His father, who, though disapproving his wild behaviour, had continued to support him, died in early 1945. Lowry was deeply moved by Arthur's death, plunging into Burrard Inlet and swimming so far out it was feared he'd drowned. His mother's death in 1950 simply left him with a sense of relief.

In 1954, Margerie, disenchanted with life in a shack, persuaded a reluctant Lowry to return to Europe. But as ever, leaving his 'Eridanus' led to drunkenness and mental breakdown. After he had attacked Margerie and had been admitted to psychiatric clinics in France and Italy, she brought him to England for treatment on the NHS. He survived courses of aversion therapy at a Wimbledon clinic, before moving to the White Cottage in Ripe. There Malcolm seemed recovered, stopped drinking and resumed work, while Margerie continued drinking. The doctor thought she was part of the problem and that a temporary separation might help, a suggestion she vehemently rejected.

On 26 June 1957, returning to the cottage from a local pub, according to Margerie, Malcolm became violent, forcing her to flee to a neighbour for shelter. Next morning she found him dead. He had taken pills, consumed half a bottle of gin and choked on his own vomit. The coroner's verdict was 'death by misadventure', but friends of Malcolm, and his brother Stuart, who travelled from Liverpool for the funeral in Ripe, were deeply suspicious of Margerie, suspecting that she had a hand in his death. She had become interested in another man and the pills Malcolm had swallowed were prescribed for her. His doctor refused to treat her and after a period in a psychiatric ward she returned to America, where she set about completing Malcolm's unfinished novels and stories and getting them published. Controversial though this was, it does mean that three novels, a novella, a book of short stories, a collection of poems and several volumes of letters are now in print – the available oeuvre of Malcolm Lowry, probably the most neglected genius of modern English literature.

Some argue that Lowry lacked imagination. Everything he wrote was based on first-hand experience, often deliberately engineered. There is something in this. He sailed for China to have something to write about, was in and out of bars and psychiatric clinics, always clutching a notebook or with something on which to scribble. Journeys to Mexico and Europe were recorded in diaries, sometimes by Margerie, and transformed into fiction. But it required a particular kind of imagination to weave his Mexican experiences into *Under the Volcano* and his Bellevue notebook into *Lunar Caustic*. What's more, his *Voyage that Never Ends* was a great imaginative project which only collapsed because his health failed.

Lowry's characters are usually in motion, usually in search of salvation of some kind – sobriety, sanity or love. He travelled to school by train, and several of his early stories take place in railway carriages. Conrad Aiken saw one version of *In Ballast* in Mexico in which he recalled a marvellously surreal account of a trip up the Manchester Ship Canal. In another, his main character describes flying over Merseyside in a small plane. His finely wrought experimental short story, 'Through the Panama', is based on a voyage through the great canal to Europe. Travel suited a prose style which could move easily between levels of consciousness in a way he had learned from Aiken and Joyce.

His poetry (some carrying Liverpudlian echoes) is uneven, sometimes flawed by an awkward line. However, several poems are memorable. Earle Birney, the Canadian poet, edited a selection of Lowry's poems for Lawrence Ferlinghetti's City Lights bookshop in 1958, and Philip Larkin included an appropriately alcoholic one in his *Oxford Book of Twentieth Century Verse*. A *Collected Poems* appeared in 1992, and some of his verse was included in Michael Hofmann's recent *The Voyage that Never Ends*. Some of the best are quite comic and worth reading aloud, especially 'Delirium in Vera Cruz' and his oft-quoted 'Epitaph', in which a self-mocking Lowry departs this life accompanying himself on the ukulele.

He certainly had poetry in his veins, and his fiction is shot through with inspired imagery. *Ultramarine*, *Under the Volcano*, *Lunar Caustic* and *Hear Us O Lord from Heaven Thy Dwelling Place* (named after an old Manx fisherman's hymn) are fine works of poetic prose. You can swim in the rich currents of Lowry's word-flows as you can in those of Joyce, Faulkner and Thomas Wolfe. His vision was always poetic and high-flown. His later stories embrace a new Lowry, no longer trawling around taverns in search of his soul, but exploring the Canadian wilderness in search of oneness with nature.

Writers claiming to have been influenced by him include Gabriel García Márquez, William Gass, Allen Ginsberg, J. G. Farrell, Robert Nye, Allan Massie, Salman Rushdie, the Cuban Guillermo Cabrera Infante, and Graham Greene, whose *The*

Honorary Consul exhibits significant parallels with the *Volcano*. B. S. Johnson's *Trawl* is greatly influenced by *Ultramarine* and, intriguingly, at the end of Luis Buñuel's film *Los Olvidos* (1950) his anti-hero meets the same end as Lowry's Consul – killed, his body tossed away with a dead dog thrown after him.

Under the Volcano has always excited film-makers. Lowry was greatly influenced by cinema and his style mimics film techniques – the flashback, the cross-cut, the voice-over – so that the novel appears to be perfect cinematic material. But its filmic history is disappointing. According to the German producer Wieland Schulz-Keil, 66 screenplays had been written for various directors before John Huston made his somewhat imperfect 1984 film of the novel. The list included Joseph Losey, for whom Cabrera Infante wrote the screenplay, and Ken Russell, who considered one with Melvyn Bragg. Luis Buñuel contemplated and finally abandoned the idea, saying, 'How can you film the inside of a man's head?'

Radio, of course, can do just that, and a superb three-hour BBC radio dramatisation of the *Volcano*, with Paul Scofield narrating and Norman Rodway as the Consul, was broadcast in 1979, with jazz accompaniment by Graham Collier. Bragg made his first BBC television documentary on Lowry with Tristram Powell, a programme which includes a host of Lowry's friends, and the Film Board of Canada made a long, haunting movie, *Volcano*, with Richard Burton as narrator. One or two novels have featured Lowry, and at least one play – Michael Mercer's *Goodnight Disgrace!*, exploring his fraught relationship with Aiken.

Malcolm Lowry's work carries many references to Merseyside. He saw Liverpool as a fascinating but blighted city. In 'Through the Panama', he quotes a visitor to Panama City saying, '[It] would be difficult to find elsewhere on the earth's surface a place in which so much villainy and disease and moral and physical abomination were concentrated.' 'He had,' wrote Lowry, 'evidently not lived in Liverpool'.[5] But for Lowry his City of Dreadful Night had played a big part in making him into the writer of genius he was.

© Gordon Bowker 2009

---

5   Malcolm Lowry, 'Through the Panama', in *Hear Us O Lord*, p. 59.

Edward Burra, *Dancing Skeletons*, 1934, gouache and ink wash on paper, 78.7 x 55.9 cm
© Tate, London, 2009

Lowry timeline

1909
28 July: Clarence Malcolm Lowry born, Warren Crest, North Drive, New Brighton, Wirral, fourth son of Arthur and Evelyn Lowry

1911
Lowry family move to 'Inglewood', Caldy, Wirral

1915
Lowry attends Braeside School, West Kirby, Wirral

1919
Lowry attends Caldicott School, Hitchin, Hertfordshire
Summer: holiday to Isle of Man

1923
Lowry attends The Leys school, Cambridge

1925
Publishes first short stories in school magazine, the *Leys Fortnightly*

1926
Falls in love with Carol Brown, to whom he writes prolific and witty letters; and then with Tess Evans ('Janet' in *Ultramarine*)

1927
With school friend Ronnie Hill, writes songs; pays for two of them to be published in London
14 May: sails to Far East from Birkenhead as deckhand on SS *Pyrrhus*. The voyage will form the basis of novel *Ultramarine*
September: returns; studies for Cambridge Entrance
December: reads American writer Conrad Aiken's *Blue Voyage*

1928
September/October: studies German in Bonn. Develops fascination with German Expressionist films. In Bonn, meets Paul Fitte

1929
Stays with Aiken in Boston, MA, as 'paying house guest'
Reads Norwegian writer Nordahl Grieg's *The Ship Sails On*
November: matriculates at St Catharine's College, Cambridge
15 November: Paul Fitte discovered dead in his rooms from gas poisoning. Lowry later claims to have helped Fitte seal up his windows while drunk; 15 November becomes a dreaded date for him

1930
Stays with Aiken in Rye, Sussex
Passes Part I of the Cambridge Tripos
August: sails on SS *Fagervik* from Preston, originally bound for Leningrad, but redirected to Aalesund, Norway; in Oslo, manages to meet Nordahl Grieg

1931
Lowry's story 'Punctum Indifferens Skibet Gaar Videre' published in *Best British Stories of 1931* under title 'Seductio ad Absurdum'

1932
Scrapes Third Class Honours from Cambridge. Lives in London.
Ultramarine accepted for publication by Jonathan Cape

1933
To Granada with Aiken and English artist Edward Burra
May: meets Jan Gabrial
June: *Ultramarine* published

1934
6 January: marries Jan Gabrial in Paris
April: Jan returns home to the US
July: Lowry sails from Southampton to New York to be with Jan
Working on *In Ballast to the White Sea* and short stories

1935
Living with Jan in New York; drinking heavily

1936
May: enters Bellevue psychiatric hospital as a voluntary patient. His experiences will form basis of novella *Lunar Caustic*
He and Jan travel across the US by Greyhound bus prior to visiting Mexico
October: arrive in Acupulco, Mexico 'on the Day of the Dead' (in fact it is two days before, on 30 October)
November: rent house at 62 Calle Humboldt, Cuernavaca, which will become setting for the Consul and Yvonne's house in *Under the Volcano*
Begins work on first version of *Under the Volcano*; originally a short story, then novella, then novel

1937
Aiken and Burra visit; Lowry drinking heavily
December: Jan leaves for LA, refusing to tolerate Lowry's drinking
Lowry spends Christmas in jail in Mexico

1938
July: Lowry returns to LA, his affairs in the hands of attorney Benjamin Parks, employed by Arthur Lowry
Working on *The Last Address [Lunar Caustic]* and *Under the Volcano*

1939
7 June: meets Margerie Bonner, an American divorcée and former actress
July: Jan files for divorce. Malcolm taken to Vancouver by Parks in order to be able to apply for a renewal of his US visa
September: Margerie joins him in Vancouver

1940
First version of *Under the Volcano* completed
August: Malcolm and Margerie visit Dollarton, on Burrard Inlet north of Vancouver, for a 'vacation'; decide to stay. Neighbours include Jimmy Craige, Manx boatbuilder
November: Malcolm receives final divorce papers
2 December: Malcolm and Margerie marry

1941
Malcolm and Margerie buy shack at Dollarton, Lowry's 'paradise' which will feature in short stories in *Hear Us O Lord from Heaven Thy Dwelling Place*. Revising *Under the Volcano*, *The Last Address* and *In Ballast to the White Sea*

1944
7 June: shack destroyed by fire. Manuscript of *Under the Volcano* rescued but that of *In Ballast...* and revision notes for *Lunar Caustic* lost

1945
11 February: death of Arthur Lowry
Rebuilding shack and building pier
Under the Volcano completed and sent to Jonathan Cape
November: fly to LA to visit Margerie's family and thence to Mexico; Margerie keen to see the setting of *Under the Volcano*
In Cuernavaca, rent apartment at 24 Calle Humboldt – Jacques Laruelle's house in the *Volcano*
December: receives letter and reader's report from Cape, offering to publish if revisions are made

1946
January: composes long letter to Cape arguing for publication of the *Volcano* as it stands
April: *Under the Volcano* accepted by Cape in London and by Reynal & Hitchcock in New York
May: returns to Vancouver
December: to New Orleans and thence Haiti

1947
February: in New York for publication of *Under the Volcano*
November: Malcolm and Margerie sail for Europe via Panama Canal
Under the Volcano published in UK
23 December: disembark at Le Havre

1948
Lowry again drinking heavily
Travel to Italy

1949
January: return to Dollarton. Working on *Dark as the Grave Wherein My Friend is Laid*, short stories in *Hear Us O Lord...*, film treatment of Fitzgerald's *Tender is the Night*

1950
May: French translation of *Under the Volcano* published
7 December: death of Evelyn Lowry

1951
Developing idea of *The Voyage that Never Ends* as over-arching scheme for his various works in progress. Working on stories for *Hear Us O Lord...*
September: German translation of *Under the Volcano* published

1952
Signs contract with Random House for *The Voyage that Never Ends*
Struggling to finish any one of multiple works; 'October Ferry to Gabriola', first conceived as short story within *Hear Us O Lord...*, expands to novella and then novel

1953
Margerie agitating to leave Dollarton on grounds of her health
October: Lowry sends first batch of *October Ferry* to editor Albert Erskine

1954
January: Random House suspend payments to Lowry
August: Malcolm and Margerie leave Dollarton for the last time
September: Lowry says a drunken goodbye to Conrad Aiken before he and Margerie sail from New York for Italy
October: in Sicily, Lowry drinking heavily

1955
July: in England
September: Malcolm admitted to Brook Hospital, London, for 'drying out'; Margerie believes he needs brain surgery, but doctors conclude there is nothing wrong
November: Lowry admitted to the Atkinson Morley Hospital, London, for psychiatric treatment, ECT and aversion therapy

1956
February: Lowry discharged from hospital and working again on *October Ferry*. Malcolm and Margerie rent White Cottage, Ripe, Sussex
31 May: Malcolm and Margerie banned from The Lamb pub in Ripe after a drunken fight
July: Malcolm readmitted to the Atkinson Morley; discharged in August
October: Margerie admitted to St Luke's Woodside Hospital, London, for psychiatric treatment

1957
Lowry working hard on *October Ferry to Gabriola*
27 May: Malcolm and Margerie leave Ripe for holiday in the Lake District, returning on 22 June
26 June: following a drunken fight, Margerie spends the night with a neighbour
27 June: Margerie finds Malcolm dead
1 July: inquest records death by misadventure; cause of death, 'swallowing a no. of barbiturate tablets whilst under the influence of alcohol'
3 July: Lowry's funeral, Ripe Parish Church

1961
Hear Us O Lord from Heaven Thy Dwelling Place published

1962
Ultramarine re-published
Malcolm Lowry Selected Poems published by City Lights Books, San Francisco, edited by Earle Birney with the assistance of Margerie

1963
Lunar Caustic published, edited by Margerie Lowry and Earle Birney

1964
Spanish translation (by Raúl Ortiz) of *Under the Volcano* published

1965
Selected Letters published, edited by Margerie Lowry and Harvey Breit
Gabriel García Márquez reads *Under the Volcano*

1968
Dark as the Grave wherein My Friend is Laid published, edited by Margerie Lowry and Douglas Day

1970
October Ferry to Gabriola published, edited by Margerie Lowry

1971
1–15 May: *Under the Volcano* dramatized by Eric Ewans (starring Paul Scofield) – first of three parts broadcast by BBC Radio 4

1976
Feature-length Oscar-nominated documentary, *Volcano: An Inquiry into the Life and Death of Malcolm Lowry*, directed by John Kramer and Donald Brittain for National Film Board of Canada

1977
Commissioned by the Ilkley Literature Festival, Graham Collier's *Day of the Dead* music/prose tribute to Lowry is premiered, featuring some of the UK's leading jazz players and narration by John Carbery. A second composition, *October Ferry & Triptych*, is premiered in Budapest

1983
Gordon Bowker recalls:
'A Saturday school under auspices of the Adult Studies Department of Goldsmiths College. Ron Binns was the speaker and the National Film Board of Canada documentary *Volcano* was shown. The projector broke down halfway through and we had to wait almost an hour for a technician to show up, but not a solitary soul left. It was the enthusiasm of that class that led me to propose a week's conference which Adult Studies also agreed to administer.'

1984
Under the Volcano filmed, directed by John Huston, starring Albert Finney. **Gordon Bowker recalls:**
'The John Huston film reported for the *Observer*, the *NY Times* and BBC *Kaleidoscope* (interviews with Huston and cast), and I did interviews for the BBC Radio 4 documentary *The Lighthouse Invites the Storm*, which provided the material for *Malcolm Lowry Remembered*. For that I spoke with Malcolm Bradbury, Anthony Burgess, Russell Lowry, Arthur Calder-Marshall, Walter Allen, James Stern, Albert Erskine, Kathleen Raine, Carole Hyde (Lowry's boyhood girlfriend), and Anna Wickham's son James – all of whom had been deeply impressed by Lowry in their various ways.'

First International Lowry Conference at Goldsmiths College, London. **Gordon Bowker recalls:** 'Muriel Bradbrook and Arthur Calder-Marshall were among the speakers. Richard Hoggart, then the College Warden, turned up, as did Michael Hastings, the playwright, who briefly considered writing a play about Malcolm and Jan, along the lines of his *Tom and Viv*. Stephen Spender was scheduled to appear but cried off at the very last moment. Melvyn Bragg came along at short notice to talk about his documentary on Lowry, *Rough Passage*, and wrote about the occasion in *Punch*. There was a meal at Bertorelli's for all the contributors, and a visit to The Fitzroy Tavern where the landlord refused a lovely photograph of Lowry which the BBC had had framed for us and which was intended for the bar-room wall to stand alongside Dylan Thomas. For the occasion we mounted an exhibition of photographs of young Lowry (donated by Russell Lowry), and Ron Binns mapped out a 'Tour of Lowry's London'.

'A couple of days before the event Calder-Marshall rang to ask me to set up a jug of water on the table for him. "But," he said, "I want you to fill it with gin. Nobody will know." And so there he sat giving his talk and sipping away merrily throughout a somewhat "fiery" discourse which began with a wonderful story about Lowry's inability to stop drinking!'

5 July: Nanaimo, British Columbia: premiere of Michael Mercer's play *Goodnight Disgrace*, a dramatisation of the relationship between Lowry and Conrad Aiken

1986
9 July: 'Laruelle's tower' in Cuernavaca is preserved by the actions of John Spencer and friends

1987
International Malcolm Lowry Symposium, University of British Columbia, Canada

1988
29 September: death of Margerie Lowry, aged 83

1989
28 July: documentary *Malcolm Lowry en México* premieres in Cuernavaca and Mexico City

1993
The Malcolm Lowry Room nightclub established by Michael Turner in Vancouver. It runs for four years

1999
Lowry conference at the Centro Nacional de las Artes, Mexico City, with Gordon Bowker, Hernán Lara and Raúl Ortiz
2002
November 2: First Malcolm Lowry International Colloquium, University of Morelos, Cuernavaca, Mexico

2006
An exhibition, *Quauhnahuac – Die Gerade ist eine Utopie (the Straight Line is a Utopia)*, curated by Adam Szymczyk at the Kunsthalle Basel, takes the Aztec name for Cuernavaca and brings together historical and contemporary artists to 'investigate the idea of journey' with reference to Lowry and *Under the Volcano*

2007
27 June: 'Malcolm Lowry: Fifty Years On' symposium, University of Sussex, followed by visit to Lowry's grave and an evening in The Lamb, Ripe
2 November: Second Malcolm Lowry International Colloquium, University of Morelos, Cuernavaca, Mexico

2008
21 February: first Lowrian Day, Cuernavaca, Mexico; showing of *The Hands of Orlac*; launch of the Malcolm Lowry Foundation blog

2009
23–25 July: Malcolm Lowry Centenary International Conference, University of British Columbia, Canada
28 July: Third Malcolm Lowry International Colloquium, Cuernavaca, Mexico
25 September–22 November: Lowry centenary arts programme presented by the Bluecoat in Liverpool

Notes on contributors

Brian O'Toole, cartoons, ink on paper,
TOP 12.5 x 15.5 cm
BOTTOM 12.8 x 11 cm

Courtesy of Catherine Marcangeli

Bryan Biggs is Artistic Director of
the Bluecoat. He was instrumental in
initiating the arts centre's recent capital
development and directs programmes of
contemporary visual arts, performance,
live art and participation. He has
curated numerous exhibitions and
international exchange programmes,
and guest curated *New Contemporaries*, two
Liverpool Biennials, and an exhibition
from Liverpool for the 2006 Shanghai
Biennale. He has written for periodicals
such as *Third Text* and *Bidoun*, essays for
exhibition catalogues, including Tate
Liverpool (*Centre of the Creative Universe*)
and *Susan Hefuna* (Verlag Kehrer,
Heidelberg), edited the revised version
of John Willett's *Art in a City* in 2007 and
companion volume *Art in a City Revisited*
(2008), and written on the intersection
of art and popular music. A fine art
graduate, he continues to maintain a
drawing practice, and has an MA in
Social Enterprise from Liverpool John
Moores University. He is the curator
of the Lowry Centenary programme in
Liverpool (2009).

Ross Birrell's solo exhibitions include
Envoy, Ellen de Bruijne Projects,
Amsterdam (2003), Bürofreidrich,
Berlin (2003), and Freismuseum,
Leeuwarden (2005). Group exhibitions
include *Greyscales/CMYK*, Tramway,
Glasgow (2002), the 4th Gwangju
Biennale, Korea (2002), *Utopia
Station*, Sindelfingen (2003), *Romantic
Conceptualism*, Kunsthalle Nürnberg/
BAWAG Foundation Vienna (2007), *Das
Gelände*, Kunsthalle Nürnberg (2008),
TIMECODE, DCA (2009). In 2007 he
was awarded a Scottish Arts Council
Artist's Film & Video Award to make
Guantanamera, a collaborative film with
David Harding. Previous collaborations
with Harding are *Port Bou: 18 Fragments
for Walter Benjamin* (2005) and *Cuernavaca:
A Journey in Search of Malcolm Lowry*,

commissioned by Kunsthalle Basel
(2006), of which the artist says: 'The
mescal-infused poetic symbolism drawn
from Dante to the Caballa, which
informed the writing of *Under the Volcano*
was the inspiration for the composition
of *Cuernavaca* – where the editing
attempts to mirror Lowry's intoxicated
syntax. The book's final lines are the
source for the installation, *You Like This
Garden?*'. Ross Birrell is represented by
Ellen de Bruijne Projects, Amsterdam.

Gordon Bowker taught at Goldsmiths
College, University of London. He has
edited three books on Malcolm Lowry:
Under the Volcano: A Casebook (1987); *Malcolm
Lowry Remembered* (1985); and, with Paul
Tiessen, *Apparently Inconspicuous Parts*
(1990). He also published a biography
of Lowry, *Pursued by Furies* (1993), which
was named a Notable Book of the Year
by the *New York Times*. Since then he
has written *Through the Dark Labyrinth: A
Biography of Lawrence Durrell* (1996) and
George Orwell (2003). Currently he is
working on a book about literary exile.
Among the publications to which he
has contributed are the *Times Literary
Supplement*, the *London Magazine*, the
Independent, the *Observer* and the *Guardian*.

Edward Burra (1905-76) occupies a
particular place in twentieth-century
British art: represented in major
collections, notably the Tate, yet as
a 'baroque modernist' remaining
something of an outsider. He is best
known for his often macabre and
satirical paintings of urban life,
particularly its seamier side in the 1920s
and 1930s – London low life, cafés in
France, Harlem street scenes and New
York night life. Though not a Surrealist,
he flirted with Surrealism, exhibiting
in the 1936 London exhibition, and
his allegorical works share some
of its characteristics. Still lives and
landscapes preoccupied him in later
years. Working mainly in watercolour
using strong colours, he imbued much
of his art with 'a feeling of tawdriness

155

and the meretricious and yet, at the same time, [created] such convincing beauty' (George Melly). Born into a wealthy family in Rye, Sussex, Burra suffered from arthritis from an early age. Despite his constant ill health he travelled widely, and with Conrad Aiken visited Lowry in Mexico in 1937. Burra and the English writer did not get on, and though no paintings from this visit survive, the artist reflected on his Mexican experience on his return to England, in works such as *Mexican Church*, circa 1938 (Tate, London).

A graduate of Goldsmiths College of Art and a member of the London Group, **Julian Cooper** is one of the most original and thought-provoking contemporary mountain painters. Son of quintessential Lake District watercolour painter William Heaton Cooper and sculptor Ophelia Gordon Bell, and grandson of the Post-Impressionist Alfred Heaton Cooper, his life has inevitably intersected with the wider currents of mountaineering and art. With work in many public and private collections, he has exhibited widely over three decades, including *Mind has Mountains* (2001), Wordsworth Trust and Art Space Gallery, London; a major retrospective at the Museo Nazionale Della Montagna, Turin (2005); and *Earthly Powers*, Art Space Gallery, London and Tullie House Museum, Carlisle (2007). *Under the Volcano* was instrumental in his search to develop a kind of abstract painting using figurative methods and capable of taking on contemporary experience in the way that Lowry's novel does. Douglas Day's biography in particular, linking Lowry's life to his fiction, provided Cooper with a 'layering of myth and reality, analogous to the early renaissance painters... I see the novel now as quite prophetic in the way that its leading metaphor applies as much to an "economic growth" as to an alcohol addiction'. His series of seven paintings entitled *Under the Volcano*, completed in the 1980s, was followed by another about the assassination of Brazilian union leader

and environmentalist Chico Mendes. Although linking formally back to the Abstract Expressionists, Cooper's current paintings of mountains, rock surfaces and marble quarries also carry forward the complex layering of meaning that he found in Lowry's masterpiece. Julian Cooper is represented by Art Space Gallery, London.

Ailsa Cox writes: 'I first read *Under the Volcano* as part of my English degree, and although it was hard to get into it's stayed in my head ever since. Lowry is probably the biggest influence on my own writing, especially the orchestration of voices and images, the layering of time and the intensity of his prose style. I'm mostly a short story writer, and my collection, *The Real Louise*, is available from Headland Press. I'm also the author of *Writing Short Stories* (Routledge) and *Alice Munro* (Northcote House). I'm Reader in English and Writing at Edge Hill University in the UK.'

Colin Dilnot is a Wirral-based writer and artist. After working in Liverpool for over 30 years in housing and social care, since 2003 he has devoted most of his time to music and art projects. He collects, records and archives information about all facets of soul music. He has published articles, hosted radio shows and contributed research to many projects dedicated to soul music in the USA, Europe and Japan. He currently runs In Dangerous Rhythm, one of the world's largest blogs dedicated to soul music. Over the last 15 years, he has produced a series of collages entitled *The Aztec Diary* exploring loss and grief. In 2008 he worked on the Hope Street Project, a laser installation connecting the two iconic cathedrals in Liverpool, and is currently working on a Liverpool-based project on communities' responses to death and loss. He has conducted research into Lowry's Wirral since the 1980s, when he first set up home near to Lowry's birthplace in New Brighton.

Annick Drösdal-Levillain teaches English at Strasbourg University, France. She started exploring the ripples and riddles of Lowry's subversively volatile writing in a PhD on *Under the Volcano* in 2001. From then on, encounters and coincidences have paved her way through what she calls the 'Lowryan echo-sytem', with a special interest in the resonances at play and the emergence of a language beyond language. She has recently focused her studies on the transfiguration of the artist's subjective past into poetic prose.

Pete Flowers lives and works in Melling, Lancashire. He trained in Fine Art at Manchester Polytechnic and Printmaking (MA) at Chelsea College of Art. He has a long career in lecturing and community arts work, and is a director and founder member of Green Close Studios. He has exhibited in major national and international galleries including the Royal Academy, Hayward Gallery, Whitechapel Gallery, Bankside and Camden Arts Centre in London; Oxford Gallery, Oxford; Cartwright Hall, Bradford; Summerville Gallery, New York; Minoa University, Egypt; Spinney's, Sharjah; Leopoldo Flores Gallery, Toluca, Mexico. He has work in public and private collections in the UK and abroad. Pete writes: 'My interest in Mexico was fuelled by reading *Under the Volcano*. It introduced me to The Day of the Dead, which became a life-long fascination. Years later I was invited to exhibit at Toluca University, and spent time in Mexico. My copy of *Under the Volcano* having long since disappeared, I bought a new edition, with an introduction by Michael Schmidt that made me aware of parallels between my work and Lowry's. Like his work, my paintings are worked over and over again, becoming more and more dense and complex. Like him I have also been drawn to the spiritual.'

Michele Gemelos was born and raised in Brooklyn, New York and is a graduate of Skidmore College. She came to Britain to study English literature at the University of Oxford. Her master's and doctoral theses focused on British writing about New York City from the late nineteenth century through the 1930s. Her first encounter with Malcolm Lowry was through *Under the Volcano*, and she soon discovered that Lowry could be added to her growing list of twentieth-century 'British New York writers' thanks to his posthumously published novella, *Lunar Caustic*. Having taught modern British and American literature at Oxford, Michele now teaches at the University of Cambridge, where she regularly recommends Lowry to her students.

Mark Goodall is a lecturer in media and communications in the Bradford Media School at the University of Bradford. He is the author of *Sweet and Savage: The World through the Shockumentary Film Lens* (Headpress) and co-editor of *Crash Cinema: Representation in Film* (CSP). He is the co-organiser of a project called 'Wild Eye: Experimental Film Studies' and is using the work of Malcolm Lowry to reinvent critical writing on cinema and other media forms. He came to Lowry by way of the radical post-war French avant-garde. Therefore, although he loves *Under the Volcano*, he is just as interested in Lowry's 'unfinished' projects and in unearthing the cosmic worlds beyond the literary canon.

David Harding writes: 'A shared passion for Mexico led me to a second awareness of Malcolm Lowry. A forgotten reading of *Under the Volcano* and my disappointment on seeing Huston's film in the past, an invitation from Adam Szymczyk, Director of the Kunsthalle Basel, to Ross Birrell and me, to think about making a film on Lowry in Cuernavaca fired a rekindling of interest. Like Lowry I moved around a lot: from Edinburgh, the

Outer Hebrides, Nigeria, Glenrothes, Dartington and finally Glasgow, to the School of Art as head of a new department, Environmental Art. Unlike Lowry I was never thrown out of anywhere but I did get into the USA illegally from Tijuana without a passport. Numerous visits to Mexico put me in the "culture zone" to say yes to the making of the film. Had Lowry published only the letter he wrote, in January 1946, to Jonathan Cape he would be worth celebrating.'

Born in Birkenhead, Adrian Henri (1932–2000) was poet, painter, performer, musician with the band Liverpool Scene, writer (including *Environments and Happenings* [1974]) and a seminal figure on the Liverpool art scene. He is best known as one of the three poets in *The Mersey Sound*, one of the bestselling and most influential poetry anthologies of all time in the UK. Henri's partner Catherine Marcangeli describes his interest in Lowry: 'He went to see the Day of the Dead exhibition at the Museum of Mankind, a visit that had immediate echoes with Lowry. He bought lots of paper-lace patterns, sweets in the shapes of skulls, and all manner of folkloric artefacts. As usual with Adrian, when he painted the Day of the Dead years later those echoes were also mixed with a host of other references, the most important and obvious one being his own *Entry of Christ into Liverpool*, of which *The Day of the Dead in Hope Street* is a kind of new version, except that the 'friends and heroes' are dead ones here. There are other echoes, of a visit we made to a graveyard in Lorraine, on the Day of the Toussaint (All Saints' Day, when everybody in France takes flowers to the graves of their dead friends or relatives, so the graveyards are incredibly colourful); also echoes of the eerie and sinister masks at the Basle Carnival, which we went to when I lived in Strasbourg in the late 1980s, and on which Adrian was planning to base a series of paintings.'

Cisco Jiménez studied in Mexico and New York. He has exhibited widely in Mexico and Latin America, US, Europe and China. His most recent solo exhibitions include Museo de Arte Contemporaneo de Guayaquil, Ecuador (2007) and Galeria Fucares, Madrid, Spain (2006). His numerous group exhibitions include *American West*, Compton Verney, Warwickshire, England (2005), *Quauhnahuac*, Kunsthalle Basel (2006), and the *22nd Annual Day of the Dead*, Lawdale Art Center, Houston (2007). Cisco writes: 'As a native of Cuernavaca, for me Lowry's book and his life provide a parameter for measuring the expectations and failures of this place. The paradox portrayed in the novel repeats again and again right in front of us: the clash of the popular against the contemporary, tradition under threat from global changes and impositions, the failure of utopianism (colonial utopias, the social experiments of the sixties, and neoliberal policies in the nineties). Cuernavaca is no longer what it used to be. What remains are tourism and opportunistic "clichés" of the quiet and colonial past – multiple thematic hotels and restaurants for wealthy foreigners and visitors from Mexico City, and real estate speculation. Nature has been covered over with tons of concrete, and the last old mansions with their majestic gardens are slowly falling down, giving way to massive condominiums (which we called "condemoniums"). You face such disaster every day. My work deals with all these contradictions.'

Related to neither fellow North West namesake Malcolm nor the Salford painter L. S. Lowry, Ray Lowry (1944–2008) nonetheless found in the former a kindred spirit, while – like the latter – he was inspired by the urban landscape of his native Lancashire. He is associated principally with punk, particularly the Clash, whom he accompanied on their 1979 tour of the US. His iconic sleeve design for their *London Calling* LP pays homage to Elvis's eponymous first album, connecting the raw energy of punk with the rock'n'roll pioneers whom Lowry admired, particularly the alluring and tragic figures of Gene Vincent and Eddie Cochran. Lowry had no formal art training, drawing cartoons in his spare time while working in advertising. Published in satirical magazines *Punch* and *Private Eye* in the '60s, his angry and anarchic drawings were also suited to the alternative UK underground press, notably *International Times*. Witnessing the Sex Pistols in Manchester on the 1976 'Anarchy in the UK' tour, his drawings took on a new urgency and became a regular feature in the *New Musical Express*, including a weekly cartoon strip *It's Only Rock'n'Roll*. Bob Dickinson observes: 'The best metaphor Ray used was to equate the over-the-top nature of rock with totalitarianism and warfare. During [Thatcherism] his humour was merciless and Swiftean' (*Guardian* obituary, 1 November 2008). Lowry concentrated on painting after music cartoon work dried up in the 1980s. He died shortly after the opening of his exhibition at his local See Gallery in Crawshawbooth. He had been working on a series of paintings inspired by *Under the Volcano*. Oasis dedicated a song to his memory during a live show in Birmingham.

Described as 'the Shirley Bassey of performance poetry' (*TES*) and 'the John Peel of poetry' (Alec Finlay), **Ian McMillan** was born in 1956 in Yorkshire where he still lives. Drummer in Barnsley's first folk-rock band Oscar The Frog, he has had a career for over 20 years as writer, performer, broadcaster, commentator and programme maker. He worked with Versewagon, the world's first mobile writing workshop, and the Circus of Poets performance poetry group. He has worked in schools, theatres, art centres, fields and front rooms, and has been poet in residence at Barnsley Football Club, Northern Spirit Trains and Humberside Police. He has written comedy for radio, plays for the stage, and has worked extensively for the BBC and Yorkshire Television. He currently presents *The Verb*, Radio 3's

Cabaret of the Word. His newest book, *The Richard Matthewman Stories*, is adapted from the Radio 4 series. Ian became excited by Lowry's life and language as a young man looking for a literary model; somehow Lowry's Mexico felt more like the centre of the universe than Barnsley, although over the years Ian has come to realise they are one and the same. Lowry's life and language still sustain the older McMillan as he chugs across Britain on trains that often slow and come to a complete halt, unlike a corpse, which will be transported by express.

Neo-Baroque printmaker and painter **Jorge Martínez García** works from his home city of Valparaíso, Chile, where he is Professor of Drawing and Painting at Pontificia Universidad Católica de Valparaíso. He studied art in Ecuador (1985–91), where he also received a BA in Philosophy. He has had 19 solo exhibitions in Chile, Ecuador, Germany, Argentina and Canada and has participated in over 40 group shows and biennales around the world. His works are in museums and major public collections in Japan, Switzerland, England, the USA, Cuba, Brazil, France, and in many private collections. The Bibliothèque Nationale de France acquired five intaglio prints in 2005. Martínez has read and re-read Lowry's writings since first discovering *Under the Volcano* in Quito. Inspired by Lowry's famous letter to Jonathan Cape, his artistic interactions with Lowry's work have been diverse and layered. The writer has always been a point of reference for Martínez's intaglio prints and paintings, and has provided motivation for reflection on Latin American realities in terms of 'our existence as culture and *cosmovision*'. Along with B. Traven and D. H. Lawrence, Lowry represents for him the outsider who is able to perceive other worlds with a universal sensibility that is at once perspicacious and profound. In his work, Martínez seeks to illuminate or, more metaphorically, to circumnavigate the 'heraldic universe'

(Lawrence Durrell) of Lowry, according to Martínez's own life experience and his existential reading of Lowry's writings. Jorge Martínez García is represented by Craig Scott Gallery, Toronto, where his most recent solo show (2007) was *Under the Volcano and Other Works: Interpreting the Writings of Malcolm Lowry*.

Nicholas Murray is a freelance author based in Wales and London. Born in Liverpool, he is the author of several literary biographies including lives of Franz Kafka, Aldous Huxley, Andrew Marvell and Matthew Arnold, two collections of poems, and two novels. He is a regular contributor of poems, essays and reviews to a wide range of newspapers and literary magazines. In 1996 he was the inaugural Gladys Krieble Delmas Fellow at the British Library Centre for the Book and he is a member of the Welsh Academy and of English PEN. He has lectured at literary festivals and universities in Britain, Europe and the United States. From 2003 to 2007 he was Royal Literary Fund Fellow at Queen Mary, University of London and is currently an RLF Advisory Fellow. *So Spirited a Town: Visions and Versions of Liverpool* was published by Liverpool University Press in November 2007 and a book about the Victorian Travellers was published by Little, Brown in April 2008. He runs a small poetry imprint, Rack Press, and writes the Bibliophilicblogger literary blog

website: www.nicholas.murray.co.uk
blog: www.bibliophilicblogger.com

Brian O'Toole (1946–2001) was, in his own words, 'hatched in Liverpool, 1946, then everything went blank'. He studied at Newcastle University (1966–70) and Goldsmiths College, London (1972–73), and thereafter spent most of his life in Kirkdale, North Liverpool, travelling frequently to Ireland where his cartoons appeared regularly in the magazine *In Dublin*. He was a James Joyce scholar and produced a highly accomplished series of portrait paintings of Irish writers. His darkly humorous, surreal pen and ink drawings appeared in a range of publications, on posters and in exhibitions, including *Punchlines* at Bluecoat Gallery (1986), which he co-curated. Frighteningly well-read, literature (as well as politics, history, philosophy and music) informed his art. He was especially drawn, like his teacher and friend Adrian Henri, to Alfred Jarry's absurd creation, Père Ubu. He was familiar with Lowry's *Under the Volcano* and its complex thematic layering, and its Day of the Dead echo in the dancing cadavers of Mexican artist José Guadalupe Posada (1851–1913), which were a particular influence.

Cian Quayle is an artist, writer and Programme Leader in Photography in the Fine Art Department at the University of Chester. Cian writes: 'I first encountered Malcolm Lowry on the bookshelves of my father, and my interest in his life and writing is concerned with the way that fact and fiction, myth, folklore and history are interwoven in narratives of exile and return. His affinity with the sea, and the idea of the journey, are pertinent in my own work and wider research. In particular Lowry's references to the Isle of Man hold a specific interest, as this is where I was born and grew up.'

Alberto Rebollo was born in Mexico City in 1972, and studied English literature at the Universidad Nacional Autónoma de México. In 2002 he won the Malcolm Lowry Prize for Literary Essays. He is about to publish *Malcolm Lowry: Between the Spell of the Volcano and a Hell of Mirrors*, edited by the Universidad Nacional Autónoma de México, where he teaches in the Departament of English. He is also president of the Malcolm Lowry Foundation of Cuernavaca, Mexico, which has organised three international colloquiums on Lowry, including a

centenary celebration. He is preparing to study for an MA at the University of Sussex.

Paul Rooney was born in Liverpool in 1967 and trained at Edinburgh College of Art. He has had residencies at Proyecto Batiscafo, Cuba and Tate Liverpool (MOMART Fellowship) and was the ACE Oxford-Melbourne Artist Fellow. He has shown recently in group projects at Tate Britain, London; Museo Reina Sofia, Madrid; Kunst-Werke, Berlin; and in the *British Art Show 6* which toured the UK in 2005–06. In 2008 he had solo shows at Matt's Gallery, London and Collective Gallery, Edinburgh and later that year won the second Northern Art Prize. Rooney now works primarily with text, sound and video, focusing on the 'voices' of semi-fictional individuals, and using or referencing narrative forms such as songs, audio guides and short stories. One of his short stories was published in a recent Serpent's Tail anthology, and a number of literary writers have influenced his recent practice, notably Malcolm Lowry. In his recent publication entitled *Wrongteous*, edited with Leo Fitzmaurice, he included an excerpt from the Lowry novella *Lunar Caustic*.

Robert Sheppard was brought up in Southwick, Sussex, and was educated at the University of East Anglia, where he was introduced to the work of Malcolm Lowry by Malcolm Bradbury on the Creative Writing MA and, at the same time, by a girlfriend's father, Mick Bailey. He now lives in Lowry's city of Liverpool, and works at Edge Hill University, where he is Professor of Poetry and Poetics. His most recent volume of poetry is *Warrant Error* (Shearsman, 2009), although his fiction appears in *Short Fiction* magazine and elsewhere. As a critic he is the author of *The Poetry of Saying: British Poetry and its Discontents* (Liverpool University Press, 2005) and *Iain Sinclair* (Northcote House, 2007).

Helen Tookey is a writer and editor, with a background in philosophy and English literature. Born in Leicester in 1969, she currently lives in Liverpool. Her publications include a monograph on Anaïs Nin, feminism and modernism (Oxford University Press, 2003) and a poetry collection, *Telling the Fractures* (Axis Projects, 2008), in collaboration with designer/photographer Alan Ward. She gave a paper ('"The Consul in the Pharmacy": Orphaned Writing, Alcohol and the *Pharmakon*-Structure in *Under the Volcano*') at the 'Malcolm Lowry: Fifty Years On' symposium at the University of Sussex in June 2007. She is grateful to Andrew Kirk for introducing her to the writing of Malcolm Lowry, which she loves for its combination of emotional power, symbolic richness and endlessly inventive language.

Michael Turner is a Vancouver writer whose fiction includes *Hard Core Logo*, *The Pornographer's Poem*, and *8x10*. He has written extensively on Vancouver art, most notably on the work of Fred Herzog, Tim Lee and Ken Lum, and has collaborated on screenplays with artists Stan Douglas and Bruce LaBruce. In autumn 2009 he begins a one-year term as writer-in-residence at Simon Fraser University, British Columbia.

certain things to get over, as you know, and it seems I have got over them. Perhaps not sufficient allowance has been made for this????? I do not any longer drink, nor, so long as I am not subjected to exhortations on the subject, do I ever feel any inclination to. This is something, as you know, upon which one has to make up one's mind oneself. I do not suppose I've had three glasses of beer in as many months, though there is plenty opportunity, much more, it turns out, than in L.A. It is not, therefore, for its dryness that I loathe Vancouver. I think you would loathe it too. It is more the stultifyingness, the boringness, the Oxford Group, the women, whom I shall never forget your referring to as looking as though they had sore feet, the fact that I have been working hard - 45,000 words since January - and that both I, and the book, badly need a change of scenery - that puts Vancouver in the dog house with me.

Finally, I do want to express my very real appreciation of what you personally have done, executively, to assist me to return to America, (and in other ways), and, while I do not feel that it is my fault in this case that at the moment it is impossible to do so, let it be perfectly understood that I certainly do not consider it yours, and that I feel only gratitude to you and a sense of personal friendship.

Yours cordially,

Malcolm.

Acknowledgements

The editors would like to thank the writers featured in this book for their enthusiastic response to our invitation. They have contributed fresh and stimulating texts, all of which were created especially for the publication.

We are indebted too to the artists for allowing us to reproduce their images, which bring a vital visual element to the book, and to others who gave permission to use images of works in public and private collections, in particular Julian and Jackie Williams at the See Gallery for sourcing original artworks by Ray Lowry, Catherine Marcangeli for permission to reproduce works from the Estate of Adrian Henri, and Craig Scott at the Craig Scott Gallery, Toronto for helping with images of Jorge Martínez García's work.

Many of the writers and artists have contributed to the project in multiple ways. Cian Quayle, Alberto Rebollo and Michael Turner provided images as well as texts. We would especially like to thank Colin Dilnot for sharing his research into Lowry's Merseyside and for supplying and sourcing images; Mark Goodall for his conceptual input, which influenced the book's structure; and Gordon Bowker for his contribution to the timeline.

We are grateful to Ken Hildebrand at the University of British Columbia Library Rare Books and Special Collections, for help in identifying and supplying photographs; and to the Liverpool Record Office for permission to use original material.

Finally we would like to thank Dave Cotterill and Robert Sheppard for early encouragement when the idea for this book was first mooted, staff at both Liverpool University Press and the Bluecoat for their support throughout, and our excellent designer, Alan Ward at Axis Graphic Design.

The Bluecoat acknowledges the support of

The City of Liverpool

Liverpool

ARTS COUNCIL ENGLAND

Supported by
ARTS COUNCIL ENGLAND